The Winter Queen & Her Legacy

The Children of Elizabeth Stuart

Beverley Adams

PEN & SWORD HISTORY

First published in Great Britain in 2026 by
Pen & Sword History
An imprint of Pen & Sword Books Limited
Yorkshire – Philadelphia

ISBN 978 1 03611 501 2

A CIP catalogue record for this book is
available from the British Library.

Typeset by Mac Style
Printed in the UK by CPI Group (UK) Ltd, Croydon, CR0 4YY.

The Publisher's authorised representative in the EU for product
safety is Authorised Rep Compliance Ltd., Ground Floor,
71 Lower Baggot Street, Dublin D02 P593, Ireland.
www.arccompliance.com

For a complete list of Pen & Sword titles please contact:

PEN & SWORD BOOKS LIMITED
47 Church Street, Barnsley, South Yorkshire, S70 2AS, England
E-mail: enquiries@pen-and-sword.co.uk
Website: www.pen-and-sword.co.uk
or
PEN AND SWORD BOOKS
1950 Lawrence Road, Havertown, PA 19083, USA
E-mail: uspen-and-sword@casematepublishers.com
Website: www.penandswordbooks.com

For David & Mary
With Much Love

Contents

Acknowledgements

As always, I would like to thank my publisher, Pen & Sword, especially Jonathan Wright, for allowing me to bring the lives of Elizabeth and her children to life. I'd also like to give a big thank you to Laura Hirst for all her patience and support during the writing of this and all my previous books.

Thank you to my family, especially my Mum, Chris and Paul. To Mary, the most wonderful auntie anyone could have wished for, who sadly passed away during the writing of this book, to her children Danielle and Luke, and to her grandchildren Faith Kai and Kali. And remembering my Dad as always.

To my wonderful friends Marie Drelincourt, Lorraine Mawdsley, Kathryn Baxendale, Amy Peat, Carol Worster, Pat Palmer and Gill Parker.

As always, a special mention and thank you to Emma Powell, who has always been unwavering in her support and encouragement for me.

Finally, thank you to all the wonderful historians who have gone before me; their work is invaluable, you may not always agree with their stance, but it is vital nonetheless.

Notes

Whilst it can be difficult to obtain accurate currency conversion rates from old money into today's figures, I have given approximate figures using The National Archives Currency Converter: 1270–2017.

In order to differentiate between Elizabeth Stuart and her daughter, I have opted to use the spelling of Elisabeth for the princess, as is often used in historical texts.

List of Illustrations

A Timeline of Events

19 June 1566	King James VI/I is born at Edinburgh Castle.
12 December 1574	Anna of Denmark is born at Skanderborg Castle, Denmark.
20 August 1589	James and Anna are married by proxy at Kronborg Castle, Denmark.
23 November 1589	James and Anna are formally married at the Old Bishop's Palace in Oslo.
1 May 1590	James and Anna arrive in Leith, Scotland.
17 May 1590	Anna is crowned Queen of Scotland at the Abbey Church of Holyrood. It is the first Protestant coronation in Scotland.
19 February 1594	Prince Henry Frederick, later Prince of Wales, is born at Stirling Castle.
19 August 1596	Princess Elizabeth, future Electress of the Palatinate and Queen of Bohemia, is born at Dunfermline Palace.
24 December 1598	Princess Margaret Stuart is born at Dalkeith Castle. She would die at Linlithgow Palace in March 1600, aged just 1 year old.
19 November 1600	Prince Charles, later Charles I, is born at Dunfermline Palace.
18 January 1602	Prince Robert, Duke of Kintyre and Lorne, is born at Dunfermline Palace. He would die aged 4 months.
24 March 1603	Elizabeth I dies at Richmond Palace. James VI of Scotland becomes James I of England and Ireland.
5 April 1603	James VI/I leaves Edinburgh for London.

7 May 1603	James VI/I arrives in London.
June 1603	Anna, Henry Frederick and Elizabeth arrive at Windsor Castle.
25 July 1603	James and Anna are crowned King and Queen of England and Ireland at Westminster Abbey.
July 1603	The 'Bye' Plot and 'Main' Plot are discovered. The Main Plot was a conspiracy by English courtiers to replace James as king with his English cousin Lady Arbella Stuart.
19 October 1603	An order is declared that Lord and Lady Harington are to take control of Princess Elizabeth's education, and she leaves court for Coombe Abbey.
4–5 November 1605	The Gunpowder Plot is foiled. Guy Fawkes is discovered in the cellars under the Houses of Parliament with barrels of gunpowder with the intention of blowing up the building during the state opening of parliament, killing James and members of his family. The plan was to place Princess Elizabeth on the throne and force her to rule as a catholic.
16 October 1612	Frederick V, Elector Palatine, arrives in London.
6 November 1612	Prince Henry Frederick dies at St James's Palace aged 18.
14 February 1613	Elizabeth and Frederick marry in the Royal Chapel at Whitehall Palace.
April 1613	Elizabeth and Frederick leave London for Heidelberg.
01 January 1614	Prince Frederick Henry is born at Heidelberg.
22 December 1617	Prince Charles Louis, later Elector Palatine, is born at Heidelberg.
23 May 1618	The start of the Thirty Years' War across Europe.
26 December 1618	Princess Elisabeth, later the Princess-Abbess of Herford Abbey, is born at Heidelberg.

2 March 1619	Queen Anna dies at Hampton Court Palace aged 44.
1619	Frederick V takes the crown of Bohemia.
4 November 1619	Frederick V is crowned King of Bohemia at St Vitus Cathedral, Prague.
7 November 1619	Elizabeth is crowned Queen of Bohemia at St Vitus Cathedral, Prague.
17 December 1619	Prince Rupert of the Rhine, later Duke of Cumberland, is born in Prague, Bohemia.
8 November 1620	The Battle of the White Mountain.
16 January 1621	Prince Maurice is born at Küstrin Castle, Küstrin, Brandenburg.
8 April 1622	Princess Louise Hollandine is born at Noordeinde, The Hague.
21 August 1624	Prince Louis is born. He would die just four months later on 24 December.
27 March 1625	King James VI/I dies at Theobalds House, aged 58.
5 October 1625	Prince Edward of the Palatinate is born at The Hague.
17 July 1626	Princess Henriette Marie of the Palatinate is born at The Hague.
16 September 1627	Prince Philip Frederick of the Palatinate is born at The Hague.
19 December 1628	Princess Charlotte of the Palatinate is born at The Hague.
7 January 1629	Prince Frederick Henry drowns at age 15 at IJ.
14 October 1630	Princess Sophia of the Palatinate, later Electress of Hanover, is born at The Hague.
14 January 1631	Princess Charlotte dies at The Hague, aged 2.
14 January 1632	Prince Augustus Adolphus of the Palatinate is born at The Hague.
29 November 1632	Frederick V dies in Mainz at age 36.
15 February 1637	Holy Roman Emperor Ferdinand II dies aged 58.

11 October 1637	End of the siege of Breda by the Dutch.
October 1639	Charles Louis taken prisoner by the French.
09 February 1641	Gustavus Adolphus dies aged 8.
23 October 1642	Battle of Edgehill, the first major battle of the English Civil War.
24 April 1645	Prince Edward marries Anna Gonzaga in Paris and converts to Catholicism.
20 June 1646	Prince Philip Frederick allegedly kills Lieutenant Colonel Jacques d'Espinay during a duel.
24 October 1648	Signing of the Peace of Westphalia brings to an end the Thirty Years' War.
30 January 1649	Charles I is executed at Whitehall, London, aged 48.
February 1650	Charles Louis marries Charlotte of Hesse-Kassel.
06 December 1650	Prince Philip Frederick is killed at the Battle of Rethel, France, aged 23.
04 April 1651	Princess Henriette Marie is married to Sigismund Rákóczi of Transylvania.
18 September 1651	Henriette Marie dies aged 25.
01 September 1652	Prince Maurice goes missing off the Caribbean coast and is presumed drowned, aged 31.
03 September 1658	Oliver Cromwell dies aged 59.
17 October 1658	Princess Sophia marries Ernst August of Hanover.
28 May 1660	The future King George I is born to Sophia, Electress of Hanover.
May 1660	Charles II is invited by Parliament to take the throne of England, Scotland & Ireland.
26 May 1660	Elizabeth Stuart arrives in England.
13 February 1662	Elizabeth Stuart dies at Leicester House, London, aged 65.
10 March 1663	Prince Edward dies aged 38.
August 1664	Louise Hollandine becomes Abbess of Maubuisson Abbey.

1667	Princess Elisabeth becomes Abbess of Herford Abbey.
28 August 1680	Charles Louis, Elector Palatine, dies aged 62.
12 February 1680	Princess Elisabeth, Abbess of Herford, dies aged 61.
21 November 1682	The future George I marries his cousin Sophia Dorothea.
29 November 1682	Prince Rupert, Duke of Cumberland, dies aged 62.
30 October 1683	The future George II is born.
26 May 1685	Charles II, Elector Palatine, dies aged 34 without issue and the Electoral Palatinate passes out of the family.
23 December 1688	James II is deposed as King of England and is replaced by Queen Mary II & her husband William III.
28 December 1694	Sophea Dorothea is found guilty of desertion and is confined to house arrest for the remainder of her life.
23 January 1698	Ernst Augustus, Elector of Hanover dies aged 68.
June 1701	The Act of Settlement is passed.
11 December 1709	Louise Hollandine, Abbess of Maubuisson Abbey, dies aged 86.
08 June 1714	Sophia, Electress of Hanover, dies aged 83.
01 August 1714	Queen Anne of Great Britain dies and George, Elector of Hanover, ascends the throne as King George I.
20 October 1714	George I is crowned King of Great Britain at Westminster Abbey.

Notable People

King James VI & I of Scotland – King of Scotland and England, father of Elizabeth Stuart.

Queen Anna – Daughter of King Frederick II and Sophia of Mecklenburg-Güstrow. Mother of Elizabeth Stuart.

Prince Henry Frederick – Eldest son of James VI/I & Anna, later became Prince of Wales. Sister to Elizabeth Stuart and brother to Charles Stuart.

Princess Elizabeth Stuart – Later Electress of Palatine and Queen of Bohemia.

Prince Charles – Later King Charles I.

Frederick V – Elector of the Palatinate, later King of Bohemia and husband of Elizabeth Stuart.

Frederick Henry – Eldest child of Frederick and Elizabeth, Hereditary Prince of the Palatinate.

Charles Louis – Son of Frederick and Elizabeth, later Elector Palatine.

Elisabeth – Daughter of Frederick and Elizabeth, later Abbess of Herford.

Charles II – Eldest child and only son of Charles Louis, later Elector Palatine.

Charlotte Elizabeth – Daughter of Charles Louis and wife of Philip d'Orléans.

Rupert of the Rhine, Son of Frederick and Elizabeth, later Duke of Cumberland.

Maurice of the Palatinate – Son of Frederick and Elizabeth.

Louise Hollandine of the Palatinate – Daughter of Frederick and Elizabeth, later Abbess of Maubuisson.

Edward, Count Palatine of Simmern – Son of Frederick and Elizabeth.

Henriette Marie of the Palatinate – Daughter of Frederick and Elizabeth.

John Philip Frederick of the Palatinate – Son of Frederick and Elizabeth.

Charlotte of the Palatinate – Daughter of Frederick and Elizabeth.

Sophia – Daughter of Frederick and Elizabeth, Electress of Hanover and heir to the British throne.

Gustavus Adolphus of the Palatinate – Son of Frederick and Elizabeth.

Ernst Augustus – Duke of Brunswick-Lüneburg, later Elector of Hanover, husband of Sophia.

George Louis, Elector of Hanover & King George I of Great Britain – Eldest child and son of Sophia and Ernst Augustus.

Princess Louisa Juliana of Orange-Nassau – Mother of Frederick V.

Maurice of Nassau, Prince of Orange – Uncle of Frederick V.

Frederick Henry, Prince of Orange – Half-brother of Maurice.

John Harington, 1st Baron Harington of Exton – Guardian of Princess Elizabeth.

Anne, Lady Harington – Wife of Sir John and joint guardian of Princess Elizabeth.

Lucy, Countess of Bedford – Lady of the Bedchamber to Queen Anna and daughter of the Haringtons.

Elizabeth Charlotte, Electress of Brandenburg – Sister of Frederick V.

George William, Elector of Brandenburg – Husband of Elizabeth Charlotte and supporter of Frederick V.

Frederick William, Elector of Brandenburg – Son of Elizabeth Charlotte and George William and supporter of the Palatinate cause.

Hans Meinhard von Schönberg – *Hofmeister* to Frederick V.

Johann Albrecht von Solms-Braunfels – Chief Advisor to Frederick V.

Ferdinand II – Archduke of Austria and Holy Roman Emperor.

Gustavus Adolphus – King of Sweden.

William Craven, 1st Baron Craven – Ardent supporter of Elizabeth.

Christian of Brunswick-Wolfenbüttel – Supporter of Elizabeth and Frederick & kinsman of Elizabeth.

Introduction

The death of Elizabeth I, Queen of England, in 1603, brought to an end the Tudor dynasty, a dynasty that her father, Henry VIII, fought so hard to prolong. Her decision not to marry brought about a succession crisis, a crisis her ministers would rather they didn't have to solve. There were various contenders to Elizabeth's crown, all of which I discuss in my previous book, *The Race for Elizabeth I's Throne: Tudor Cousins at War* (Pen & Sword 2025). In the end, the successor was James VI of Scotland, who had been king north of the border since 24 July 1567, when his mother, Mary, Queen of Scots, had been forced to abdicate in favour of her 13-month-old son. By 1603, James had been king for thirty-six years, although he was forced to rule under a Regency for many of them. He had also outlived many of his rivals for the English throne, including his mother, whom Elizabeth executed in February 1587 after spending the best part of two decades as the English queen's prisoner.

James's arrival in England heralded the start of the Stuart dynasty, a dynasty that would rule England for 110 years, after which the fiercely Protestant nation would look to the House of Hanover for its next monarch. But during those 110 years, the House of Stuart faced many upheavals, including the near extinction of the monarchy altogether. As the English Civil War raged, Charles I lost his head and England became a republic under the leadership of Oliver Cromwell. The glorious restoration of his son, Charles II, in 1660 saw the city of London celebrate, whilst the reign of his brother James II ended in disaster when he fled the country, and his crown, over arguments regarding religion. The Glorious Revolution of 1688 saw William of Orange and his wife, James II's daughter, Mary, take the throne as joint rulers. Sadly, their marriage ended childless, as did that of her sister Anne, who, despite many pregnancies, did not see any of her children live beyond childhood.

But how did England end up with a German Hanoverian ruler named George on the throne? Well, we must look back to James and his daughter Elizabeth. Elizabeth Stuart was married to Frederick V, Elector of the Palatinate, in 1613, and it is through their daughter Sophia that the monarchical line has run through ever since. Sophia was married to Ernst, Elector of Hanover and that marriage produced seven children who lived beyond adulthood. The eldest of those children was a son named George. With the death of Queen Anne's only surviving child, Prince William, Duke of Gloucester, in 1700 at the age of 11 years old, Britain knew it was facing yet another succession crisis and like in 1603, religion played a part in who would successfully and peacefully take its throne. The Act of Settlement of 1701 was passed, which meant the English and Irish throne could only pass to a Protestant. At that time, Scotland and England were still separate sovereign countries and therefore this Act did not apply north of the border.

Just as it was in 1603, a Catholic monarch would not be tolerated and if you converted or married a Roman Catholic, then you were barred from taking the crown, so a legitimate protestant had to be found. There were approximately 50–70 other claimants who came before George, including the descendants of James II and other members of the Stuart family, both at home and across Europe. The most senior claimant was that of James Francis Edward Stuart, the son of James II via his second wife, Mary of Modena. He was also the father of Charles Edward Stuart, or Bonnie Prince Charlie, as he is perhaps better known to us. He led the Jacobite rising of 1745, which failed and with that, the Stuart claims to the throne ended. All these claimants had an arguably better bloodline than George but they had one problem: they were all Catholics and such was the hatred against them that the government of England decided to weaken the bloodline and place an unknown German prince on its throne.

Princess Sophia, Electress of Hanover, was the eldest surviving child of Elizabeth Stuart and she was a Protestant. She was named heiress presumptive to the throne in 1701. On 1 May 1707, the Act of Union was passed and this united the parliaments of England and Scotland under the name of Great Britain. Following the Act of Union in 1707, Sophia was now heiress to Scotland too but sadly, she died less than two months before Queen Anne and never realised her dream of becoming queen. But like most things, it passed to her eldest son, who took the throne as King George I and with that came the dawn of the Georgian period.

On their website, the Royal Museums Greenwich describes Elizabeth Stuart as a 'hidden figure of British history', but her life was one of huge importance both at home in Britain and across Europe. Her children continued her legacy through the Hanoverian line. She fought for the protestant cause across Europe and became an influential figure, even after her husband had died. Elizabeth was a woman with many titles, but first and foremost, she was a dutiful daughter, wife and mother and her life, and those of her children are sewn into the fabric of history.

An Author's Note
The Thirty Years' War

This book focuses primarily on the lives of Elizabeth Stuart, her husband Frederick V, Elector Palatine, and their children, but much of their married life was spent intertwined with a series of battles, sieges and conquests that took place from 1618 to 1648, which became known to history as the Thirty Years' War. The reasons for the war are varied, but it was primarily down to religion, dynastic opportunities and the expansion of boundaries. The origin of the war is based on the future Holy Roman Emperor Ferdinand II, who at the time held the title of the King of Bohemia. He planned to impose Catholicism across his domains, forcing a retaliation from the Protestants of Bohemia and Austria. Other monarchs saw their opportunity to make land grabs, especially in the German states. King Christian IV of Denmark was keen to claim territory held by Sweden, but the Danes were defeated and saw them leave the war altogether. The victory on the battlefield handed Sweden even more land. Poland looked to extend its boundaries by attacking and conquering parts of Russia.

Ultimately, the war was between the Catholic Habsburgs and the German Protestant principalities who relied heavily on Sweden, England and the Dutch Estates. Many of the battles took place on German soil and saw villages, towns and farms plundered, leaving vast areas devastated and the people destitute. The war was finally brought to an end by the Peace of Westphalia in 1648. It saw Spain (the Habsburgs) lose much of its power having suffered the loss of the Netherlands and other member states of the Holy Roman Empire were granted full sovereignty. The idea of a Catholic Empire was abandoned as modern Europe began to emerge.

A list of the key battles can be found in Appendix Three.

The Mother

Part I

1566–1603

Born in 1566 at Edinburgh Castle, James Charles Stuart became king at just 13 months old following the abdication of his mother, Mary, Queen of Scots. Scotland had been, and still was, a difficult place to govern at the best of times, but it would have proved to have been more challenging with an infant on the throne. Therefore a regent was appointed, the man chosen was James's uncle, the Earl of Moray. With his mother deposed and his father, Lord Darnley, dead, James was placed into the care of the Earl and Countess of Mar at Stirling Castle with the Earl's brother, Alexander Erskine, Master of Mar, responsible for the young king's security. James was brought up alongside Erskine's sons, with whom he became close friends.

Despite living behind the secure walls of Stirling Castle, James was constantly under threat of kidnapping. When his mother escaped imprisonment at Lochlevan in May 1568, Regent Moray ordered Stirling Castle to be fortified further to ward off the threat of attack. Queen Mary's supporters tried to capture the young king but when those plans failed they switched their attention to James's guardians. But political and royal life in Scotland was not easy. There were power hungry men and a young king who was an easy target, one that could be manipulated for their own benefit In 1570, James's uncle, the Earl of Moray, and Regent of Scotland, was assassinated in Linlithgow. The following year, Moray's replacement, James's paternal grandfather, the Earl of Lennox, was fatally wounded following an attack in Stirling. He was carried back to the castle where the 4-year-old king watched on as his grandfather bled out from a stab wound to his stomach and breathed his last. The third Regent, the Earl of Mar, did not survive long after being appointed to the post; in 1572, he also died. He had attended a banquet at the home of the Earl of Morton and died shortly after. The fourth Regent was Morton; read into that what you will.

As death and uncertainty surrounded James he continued to be instructed in his studies by the Calvinist scholar George Buchanan. Despite his hatred of Queen Mary, he diligently taught him theology, history and languages including Latin and French. Alongside these academic subjects, James was taught to dance, ride a horse, archery and hunt. Buchanan's hatred of the Queen caused him to treat James harshly. He would regularly beat him as a way of punishment, for his sins and for those of his mother. Buchanan was warned over his treatment by the Countess of Mar but his response was 'I have whipped his arse, you can kiss it if you like'. He was certainly not a friend to James but he was a good tutor and through him the young boy developed a lifelong love of literature and a constant desire to learn. Buchanan did not believe in absolute monarchy and tried to make James understand that his powers as king were limited.

Buchanan's harsh treatment and attitudes did not adhere James to his tutor but he did learn well and by the age of 11 the king announced he was ready to rule Scotland by himself. Morton stepped aside relinquishing the Great Seal and the Honours of Scotland on 28 March 1578 but his supporters were not as keen to cede power to a young boy so they laid siege to Stirling Castle in an attempt to seize the king. Alexander Erskine tried his best to protect James and even lost his eldest son in the ensuing battle; James was terrified and began pulling at his hair in distress so frightened in case Erskine was killed. Erskine wasn't killed but did have to leave the castle, handing custody of the king back to Morton, leaving the country sat on the brink of civil war. By late 1578 at the age of 12, James once again declared himself fit to rule but he was alone, he had no immediate family to turn to and no one he could trust. But he had a French relative called Esme Stuart, he was a first cousin of James's father Lord Darnley and his appearance in Scotland thrilled the 13-year-old James who quickly made Stuart the Earl, and then Duke, of Lennox.

A dukedom was all well and good but Lennox, aged 37, had his eyes on a much bigger prize, he wanted the role of Regent and James was far too enthralled to the exotic Frenchman to say no. By this point James was ruling by himself so he may not have gone as far as creating him the Regent but he did appoint him to the Privy Council and showered him with gifts including titles and jewels that once belonged to his mother. But the power soon went to Lennox's head and before long he had set his sights on Morton and, along with some of his associates, had the Earl tried and executed for treason in 1581.

Unsurprisingly, Lennox was not a popular figure amongst the Scottish nobles, he was a Catholic and even though he had publicly converted to the Church of Scotland, they remained suspicious of him. He also caused alarm to the Scots who supported an alliance with England as there was always a chance he could reignite the Auld Alliance with France, which would have been a cause of great concern to Elizabeth I and England. The nobles' biggest issue with the Frenchman was his power and influence over the young king, introducing him to foul language, alcohol, women, and, according to some reports, men. The spell had to be broken, and so the leading nobles arranged a coup d état.

James was a keen hunter so it was never difficult to lure him into the saddle. On this particular occasion, the king had been told to try hunting at Ruthven Castle, near Perth, where there were supposedly plenty of deer to track. He eagerly agreed and on 23 August 1582, William Ruthven, Earl of Gowrie, along with other leading lords lured their king into a trap that became known as the Raid of Ruthven. The group managed to detain the king and when it became apparent he had been fooled James began to cry at his misfortune. He was moved to Falkland Palace and would remain confined there for the best part of a year. Once the kirk had agreed the action taken by the lords against James was justified, Lennox was ordered to leave Scotland immediately. He went back to France where he died in 1583, supposedly leaving his embalmed heart to James. James would always remain loyal to his Lennox cousins and even instructed his son Charles I to ensure they were well provided for, which he did.

James had been captured whilst hunting and it would be his favourite pursuit that would lead to his escape. Throughout the term of his imprisonment, he had earned the trust of his captors and managed to convince them he was loyal and obedient to them. When he was sure he had earned their trust, James requested the liberty to hunt, they agreed and the king made his escape from Falkland Palace on 27 June 1583. Following his escape, James started to strengthen his grasp on the crown. He managed to force through the Black Acts which saw the presbyteries brought to heel and abolished and the Kirk back under royal control with just two bishops, of which James had to power to appoint. The Black Acts were met with strong opposition, James believed in the Divine Right of Kings, answerable only to God, the teachings of Buchanan had clearly not sunk in with the young king, the Kirk however, saw him as any other member of the congregation. By 1592, James was forced to concede that the General Assembly ought to have overall control of the Church and the presbyteries but James did retain some of his authority. Like many countries across Europe at this time, religion was a controversial subject and keeping all your subjects happy was a difficult task to achieve.

James was angry following his kidnap and wanted to punish those that he felt were the main perpetrators. Even though the lords defence was that they were only trying to save James from bad influences the very fact they had forced him to banish Lennox meant he wanted his revenge. The leading lords and Presbyterian ministers who had a hand in his imprisonment were called upon to answer for their actions. Gowrie, as the ring leader, was arrested at his house in Dundee, the town had been ordered by their king to take up arms against Gowrie should he fail to surrender, which he finally did after a 12-hour siege. From Dundee he was taken to Holyrood and from there on to Stirling where his trial was held. He was found guilty of leading the Raid of Ruthven and was executed by beheading on 3 May 1584 at Stirling Castle. All his lands and titles were forfeited to the crown although the title would be restored to his son in 1586. The other culprits were banished from Scotland after a failed attack on Stirling Castle with many going to Newcastle in England.

James was always one to have favourites, Lennox was his first with the second being James Stewart, Earl of Arran. Arran was a powerful man and one that had many privileges bestowed on him by James for his loyalty during the Raid of Ruthven. He was made keeper and governor of Edinburgh Castle and lieutenant-general of the royal army, he was also given many properties by the king including the fortress Dirleton Castle in East Lothian. Arran's power and position as the leading noble was undermined and ultimately ended in July 1585 when one of his men was involved in border raids with England during which Francis Russell, son of the Duke of Bedford was fatally shot by one of Arran's men. Arran stood accused of being involved with the English which incensed James so much that he even offered to send Arran to England as a prisoner. Instead, he was imprisoned at St Andrew's Castle in Fife before being placed under house arrest at Kinneil House. At the time of the arrest, James was trying to build a strong Anglo-Scottish relationship, which was now in jeopardy of being destroyed.

Arran's imprisonment meant that he was powerless to stop the banished lords from returning and seizing Stirling Castle on 4 November 1586 where they all declared him a traitor. Arran managed to dodge the executioners axe and banishment, instead he retired to the Ayrshire countryside however, James remained loyal to him and the pair continued to communicate with each other. He returned briefly to Holyrood to meet Queen Anna. He was murdered on 5 December 1595 by Sir James Douglas of Parkhead, a nephew of Regent Morton, at the small South Lanarkshire Village of Symington.

James knew he had to do something if he was ever going to stabilise his realm and rule as its king. The last attempt on James's person took place following skirmishes where he was assaulted by Alexander Ruthven by 1600. Ruthven, brother to the Earl of Gowrie and both sons of the 2nd earl who was executed by James following the Raid of Ruthven, had managed to convince James to visit Gowrie House where Alexander had held a 'pot of gold' for James to inspect that the earl supposedly knew nothing about. The king dismissed his men and went alone, thankfully they thought better of it and followed James. Ruthven had supper with James and then invited him to go upstairs to in the tower which the king did, although he seemed to have missed the fact that every door he went through was bolted behind him. When he reached the upper part of the tower there was an unknown man sat with a dagger in his hand waiting for James to arrive. James made a move to leave but before he could Ruthven took him from behind. James tried to offer pardons and promises if they were to let him leave but it was of no help, they had only murder and revenge on their minds. James somehow managed to get to the window and shouted down 'Treason!' to his men that had followed him. They ran up the stairs breaking down each door they came to but 13-year-old page, John Ramsey found another way in and when he burst into the tower room he wasted no time in running Ruthven through with a sword. Gowrie had assured the other guests the king had already departed, when they went to see what the commotion was all about the earl and his men were met by fighting, Gowrie was fatally stabbed. Many have questioned the validity of this story but James stuck to his version of events. The mystery man turned out to be Andrew Henderson who, rather surprisingly, was pardoned by James after he had confirmed the kings version of events. But had James concocted this story as a way of ridding himself of men he had a deep hatred for? It was possible, why else would the king have willingly followed his enemy from the hunt to his house and then in to a chamber high up in a tower? Perhaps Ruthven and Gowrie, although he seems to have been out of the loop on this, were hoping to lure James into providing the family with lucrative posts at court. If that had been the case, however, why take him up a tower to a room with a man and a dagger? James had a deep-rooted fear of being trapped and held prisoner so it is little wonder he panicked, if Ruthven did have a plan to appeal to James's kind nature then he went about it the wrong way and it back fired spectacularly.

Back to 1586 and James decided he was ready to rule solely and no further attempts were made to have a Regent rule for him. He signed the Treaty of Berwick with England which brought peace to Scotland along with a pension of £4,000 for James. Also, Elizabeth agreed not to obstruct, oppose or hinder his claim to her throne. The following year Elizabeth executed Queen Mary who had been her prisoner for the best part of 20 years. The Scottish queen had been found guilty of treason after evidence was found linking her to a catholic plot that would depose Elizabeth and place her on the throne instead. The death of Mary also cleared the final obstacle that stood in James's way of claiming the English throne, that said he did try and intercede on his mother's behalf but sadly his pleas went unheard and his mother died on 8 February 1587 at Fotheringhay Castle, Northamptonshire. Following a retelling of his mother's last few hours it is said that James never mentioned her again.

James had finally become a man capable of ruling his kingdom, albeit with the assistance of his advisors, and whilst he had brought stability to Scotland, his personality was changing. His language had grown coarse and filthy and he had become a little too fond of alcohol. But perhaps the most alarming thing was he had started to surround himself with handsome young men which raised worrying questions about his sexuality. Despite being outspoken about homosexuality in public it was clear the king's preferences were leaning towards young men. Being a homosexual in sixteenth century Scotland was illegal and considered a serious crime so for there to be rumours that the king was homosexual was more than concerning. One of the most important duties of any king was to produce a legitimate heir to the throne, so the hunt began to find the Scottish king a wife.

There had been various discussions over an appropriate match but it was Frederick II of Denmark that made the first move when he sent his ambassadors to the Scottish court in 1585. Negotiations for a marriage with the Danish princess Elizabeth didn't get off to the best start when James point blank refused to return the previously Danish owned Orkney and Shetland Isles as part of the marriage treaty. However, in 1586 James arranged for portraits to be swapped but the Danish king was not happy at what appeared to be James dragging his feet. As a result, Princess Elizabeth was married elsewhere and James was told if he wanted to marry into the Royal House of Oldenburg he would have to settle with the king's younger daughter, Anna. A match with Denmark would certainly have been lucrative for James and Scotland given the Danish king was also ruler of Norway and collected vast revenues across both kingdoms. But once again any negotiations were going to be hampered by the ownership of the Orkney and Shetland Isles, Frederick was determined to see them back under Danish rule, James on the other hand was adamant they were to remain Scottish. A Danish marriage was looking highly unlikely unless the two kings could broker a deal that suited both.

A breakthrough finally came in 1588 when King Frederick died at the age of 55 leaving his 11-year-old son Christian to take the throne. Given his young age, Christian IV of Denmark and Norway required a regency council to rule for him until he came of age. His mother, Queen Sophia of Mecklenburg-Schwerin, was hoping to rule as his regent but she had been all but excluded from politics by her husband which meant the Rigsrådet had no other option but to exclude her from the regency council. But Sophia was a stubborn woman and she dug her heels in until finally the Rigsrådet caved in and appointed her guardian of her son. In July 1589 Queen Sophia finally entered the fray and finalised the details that finally sealed the deal for a marriage between Princess Anna and James. The issue of the Orkney Isles was not that important to Sophia but what was important was her daughter being married to a man of high status and you can't get much higher than a king. Given her husband had only managed to match their eldest daughter with a Duke, this was quite a coup for Sophia, especially as James may one day be king of England too. With these issues now resolved the marriage could go ahead. Anna was 14 years old and besotted with her soon-to-be husband King James. The fact he preferred the company of men was kept from the princess especially as she had fallen head over heels in love with a man she had never met. From James's perspective, he was a king and a king needed heirs, the preservation of the Stuart line was of utmost importance to king and country and he wasn't opposed to marriage, he may have enjoyed the company of men but he also enjoyed the company of women too.

The wedding took place by proxy on 20 August 1589 at Kronborg Castle (known to us as Elsinore in Shakespeare's *Hamlet*) with George Keith, 5th Earl Marischal standing in for the king. Once the ceremony was done, Keith escorted Anna to the richly decorated bridal bed upon which he lay beside her to indicate the marriage was now complete. James was keen to have his new bride on Scottish soil and Anna was just as eager to please so within ten days of the ceremony the new Queen of Scots set sail for her new home. Amongst her fleet were eighteen warships and at its head sailed the *Gideon* which was being led across the North Sea by Danish Admiral Peder Munk. Along with Munk, Anna sailed with some of Denmark's elite. Unfortunately, her first attempt had to be abandoned due to storms which saw two of her ships collide and the *Gideon* spring a leak forcing Anna and her fleet back towards the Norwegian coast. She would try several more times to put to sea but each time she was beaten back by gales. She decided to abandon her attempts until the spring and headed in land where she took up residence in Oslo. Back in Scotland James was starved of news and was becoming more than concerned for his queen's safety and was growing increasingly impatient to have his wife on Scottish soil. Despite the tempests that were blowing across the North Sea, a part of the Danish fleet did make it to Scotland; Lord Dingwall had managed to land at Leith and explained how a great storm had separated the flotilla and he thought Anna's life was at risk at sea. Panicked by this news, James ordered prayers to be said across Scotland whilst he kept watch across the Firth of Forth at Seton Palace which was ideally placed to spot any ships on the horizon. In October, news finally arrived from Anna. She had written to explain why she had abandoned her numerous attempts to cross the North Sea. She explained storms had forced her ships back each time they tried to sail and with winter approaching fast it looked doubtful she would arrive any time before spring.

King James was not willing to wait until spring to claim his wife, he was young and wanted her with him so he set sail from Leith with a retinue of over 300 to personally bring his queen home. This was his opportunity to be the chivalrous prince who was willing to risk his own safety for the love of his queen. It was a brave move on his part given the weather conditions and certainly shows a side of James that over time appears to have been replaced with one of a cowardly king. When news filtered through the court that these were his intentions, Bothwell and Lennox both formally aired their reluctance to support his ideas. His people did not wish to see their king risk his life sailing the perilous North Sea so James wrote an open letter to the people of Scotland in which he justified his reasons, rumours of his same-sex relationships had been circulating for some time so his eagerness to claim his wife was a clever ploy to put down the accusations of homosexuality once and for all. He was keen on having a family and providing his people with an heir to the throne. Finally, he bid Scotland goodbye and willed his people live in peace until the time of his return. He then set a regency council in place with Lennox as its chief councillor and made the journey to Leith.

He sailed from Scotland in late October and embarked on a four-day crossing arriving on the freezing Norwegian coast at Flekkefjord. From there the king and his retinue travelled northeast towards the town of Tonsberg where he stayed for six days. Tonsberg lay approximately sixty-three miles from Oslo meaning James had to travel over the frozen land to reach the capital, where he arrived on 19 November. The king was provided with an opportunity to freshen up his travel-stained clothes before being introduced to his bride, but in his chivalric mood, he declined this offer and instead made straight for Anna's apartments at the Old Bishop's Palace where he was promptly introduced to his new wife. His first impressions of Anna would have been favourable; she is described as being tall and slim with fine golden hair and pale skin. But what of James? He is often described as being bowed-legged, stooped with a tongue too big for his mouth meaning he drooled when he spoke. If this is true then Anna did not seem to mind. It is likely she was greeted by a tall slim man who had inherited his father's piercing blue eyes and his mother's height and together they made an attractive couple. That said, Anna did refuse his attempts to kiss her as was the Scottish custom because it was against hers.

The royal couple were finally married in the great hall at the Old Bishop's Palace in Oslo on 23 November 1589 in a ceremony officiated in French, that being the only language they shared, by David Lindsay (later Bishop of Ross). It was a lavish affair with over 300 tailors having been employed to make Anna's wedding gown alone. Her servants had fresh new liveries made and a solid silver coach had been custom built for Anna. This was clearly a plot by Denmark-Norway to show the political world they were wealthy and successful and that their princess was worthy of the title of queen. Over the following days, the newlyweds hunted and feasted together seemingly enjoying each other's company. James showed his love for Anna by bestowing on her the lands of Dunfermline Abbey and the palaces of Falkland and Linlithgow, these formed part of Anna's jointure, or 'morrowing gifts' as per the Scottish custom. Rather than return home to Scotland, James and Anna accepted an invitation to join the court of her brother, Christian IV, in Copenhagen. This would mark the beginning of a warm and friendly relationship between the two nations, and later England. Safe passage was granted for the couple to travel through Sweden where they were even given a 300-strong guard through King John's lands. When they finally arrived, James was taken into the embrace of a warm loving family, something he had never experienced. He gave Anna a crown, but in return, she had given him a stable family, and to please his new family he married Anna for a third time on 21 January 1590, this time in the Lutheran rites.

James had thoroughly enjoyed his time away from Scotland but the inevitable had to happen. In February he wrote home to advise his people should prepare for his return. The palaces of Holyroodhouse, Linlithgow and Stirling Castle were to be made ready and ships were to be ordered to carry the king and queen home. Anna had to be prepared to leave her home and her mother made sure her daughter was well taken care of and that she be received in the manner of a queen. She requested Maitland oversee the setting up of her household. James and Anna boarded the much-repaired *Gideon*, led once more by Peder Munk, which sailed at the head of a thirteen-strong fleet consisting of both Scottish and Danish ships. This would have been a moment of mixed emotions for James, he had enjoyed his time abroad, it had been one of the happiest periods of his life, free from the constraints of warring Scottish nobles he may have been reluctant to return. He had absorbed the Danish-Norwegian hospitality which probably contributed to his love of alcohol and he had enjoyed court life in Denmark amongst his new family. For Anna, she was to say goodbye to her homeland and family but on the other hand, was about to embark on a new life as a queen, a position a second daughter could only dream of. As they sailed away from Denmark, they had each other to lean on but what awaited them in Scotland neither of them could be sure.

The fleet arrived safely at Leith in the afternoon of 1 May 1590. Anna had brought with her over 200 people including her two ladies Catherine Schnickel and Anna Sophia Kaas. Having her own people around her would undoubtedly help the young queen settle into her new life in a strange country where she would have to learn the language and customs quickly. Her education started on the quayside when she was introduced to the newly defunct Regency Council, they were closely followed by the peers of the realm. This was the time to make a good impression, Anna was keen to get off to a good start with her husband's subjects but they too were keen for Anna to notice them. Many noble men had daughters or sisters that he would want to advance by getting her a place in the new queens household. Unfortunately, Anna quickly gained a reputation for not liking many of the Scots she met and would form many bitter feuds over the coming weeks and months.

The king and queen made their grand entrance into Edinburgh on 6 May. Anna travelled with her ladies in the solid silver coach which was pulled by eight fine horses whilst James rode alongside with Bothwell, Lennox and Lord Hamilton. Once they reached Holyroodhouse, Anna was taken to her luxurious apartments all of which had been recently refurbished with red velvet and cloth of gold and silver.

Anna was crowned at Holyrood Abbey on 17 May 1590 in a ceremony that lasted over seven hours. James led the first procession, dressed in rich purple velvet trimmed with ermine, he made his way from the palace to the Abbey Church next door. He was followed by his household, the nobility and then the clergy. Anna made the short journey with her Danish nobles, Scottish Lairds, the burgesses, the Lyon Herald, Sir David Lindsay and Chancellor Maitland, who had the honour of carrying the queen's crown. Anna was flanked by her Danish ladies along with the dowager Countess of Mar, Lady Seton and Lady Thirlestane. Her Danish dignitaries included Pedar Munk. Inside the Abbey, the ceremony began with Robert Bruce anointing Anna with oil on her breast and arm following this Lennox, Hamilton and her ladies escorted Anna to a private chamber where she donned her coronation robes. James then passed the crown to Lennox, who in his position as Scotland's premier peer, along with Chancellor

Maitland placed the crown upon her head. Hamilton passed her the sceptre whilst the 9th Earl of Douglas presented her with the sword of state. Anna made her oath to defend the true religion and worship God. The feasting that followed was extravagant and lasted for days but once the excitement had died down and the celebrations were over, it was time for Anna to get down to the business of queenship and the main duty she had to perform was to give James and Scotland an heir.

It took Anna three years to conceive her first child but given her young age that was not unexpected. Her pregnancy was confirmed and Stirling Castle was made ready. Amidst huge expectation and excitement Anna arrived there, escorted by James, in December 1593 when she entered confinement. There were strict rules to follow for any royal or noble woman when she was about to give birth. She usually entered her confinement 4–6 weeks prior to her delivery date and all except one of the windows of the birthing chamber were sealed shut and covered. The walls were draped in thick rich tapestries creating a dark warm room that was strictly a female-only zone. She was to remain sealed in that unpleasant atmosphere until she gave birth. Anna's moment of glory came on 19 February 1594 when she gave birth to a healthy boy. He was named Henry Frederick after his grandfathers and took the titles of Duke of Rothesay, Earl of Carrick, Baron of Renfrew, Lord of the Isles and Prince and Great Steward of Scotland. Once James had been told, a herald stepped out on to the freezing walls of Stirling Castle and announced the news to those gathered below. Scotland had waited over three years for the birth of an heir and they were elated, the country celebrated and gave thanks for the safe arrival of their prince and the good health of the queen, this little boy was the hope of the country and his father.

James sent out messengers across Scotland, down into England and across to Europe, and especially to Denmark, to tell them about his son's safe arrival. He then set about arranging his prince's christening and looked south of the border and to his own godmother, Queen Elizabeth I, in the hope she would do him the honour of performing the role for his son, she agreed. The date for the ceremony was set for 30 August 1594, Elizabeth sent the Earl of Sussex as proxy and Duke Henry Julius and

Duke Ulrich joined him as fellow godparents along with many Danish ambassadors. The lavish christening was presided over by the Bishop of Aberdeen; baby Prince Henry was collected from his mother's apartments and carried in ceremony to the newly built Chapel Royal at Stirling Castle.

Despite the joy surrounding Henry's birth cracks in the royal marriage had begun to show and they were about to become so deep it threatened the king and queen's relationship. James announced just forty-eight hours after Henry Frederick's birth that the infant prince was to be taken from his mother and raised at Stirling Castle by John Erskine, Earl of Mar and his mother Annabel, the dowager Countess. James had stipulated to the Mars that under no circumstances were they to release the prince into anyone's keeping without his authority. If he should die then they were keep custody of the prince until he reached his majority at the age of 18. The queen was incandescent with rage; she understood that royal babies were raised by nurses and guardians but they were usually kept close by in the royal household near to their mothers should they be needed. It is clear Anna's maternal instincts were raging but she also realised it put her in a politically vulnerable position as she was being openly slighted by her husband given that Stirling Castle had been the residence of at least two previous queen consorts (Margaret Tudor & Marie de Guise) where they had full access to their children. That said their husbands James IV and James V respectively, had died young and the guardianship of their young sons lay with their mothers. So why was James openly denying his wife's right to raise her son? He cited safety reasons; Scotland was a volatile country, it always had been and Stirling Castle provided a safe place for a prince to grow up, just like he had. It did not take too long before James was proved right. On 5 March the Catholic earls of Huntley, Bothwell, Erroll and Angus plotted to kidnap the prince, and using Huntley's wife Henrietta, reunite him with his mother. When James heard of their plans he ordered them to be arrested and kept under house arrest, which they flatly refused to do but James failed to take any further action against them. Before long, the court was divided, on the one hand you had the king and the Mars and on the other was the queen and her supporters.

James's decision put the Mars in Anna's firing line proved worrying as she soon began plotting their downfall with her enemy Maitland, who just so happened to despise Mar too. James got wind of her plan and ordered Maitland and Mar to publicly reconcile, which they begrudgingly did, although Maitland planned to continue encouraging Anna in her plans and thereby wreck the fragile marriage even further. A marital breakdown seemed likely when news reached Anna that James had taken a mistress called Anne Murray. But that didn't seem to stop them doing their duty and Anna soon fell pregnant again with the news becoming common knowledge in May 1595.

Things were different this time, she had spent much of her pregnancy ill but James still sent her to Stirling Castle for the birth, although Mar was under strict instructions not to hand over Prince Henry to his mother. Whether she even saw her son is disputed but the upset caused by James treatment of her along with an underlying illness caused Anna to miscarry her baby in the July. Maitland died on 3 October 1595 after a short illness marking the loss of a fine political mind leaving James without a Lord Chancellor and Anna without a co-conspirator, she would have to look elsewhere for support against Mar.

James and Anna may have been at odds over the upbringing of their son but the one thing they did have in common was the success of the succession with both being committed to providing Scotland, and more than likely England, with an heir and they had no problem conceiving with Anna giving birth another four times over the next eight years. Sadly, a daughter called Margaret born in December 1598 would die at the age of 1 year old whilst a younger brother Robert would die at just 4 months old in May 1602.

Not long after suffering her miscarriage, Anna fell pregnant again and on 19 August 1596 she gave birth at Dunfermline Palace in the Kingdom of Fife to a healthy daughter who they named Elizabeth. She was baptised by David Lindsay at Holyrood in a low-key and rather drab ceremony, gone was the glitz and glamour of her elder brother's christening. That said, Elizabeth I stood as her god-mother although the English Ambassador, Robert Bowes, stood as proxy for the queen. The

English queen never sent a gift for her new goddaughter but the city of Edinburgh donated 10,000 marks for her future dowry. The Lyon Herald then proclaimed her 'Lady Elizabeth, the first Daughter of Scotland!'. Unlike Henry, Elizabeth seems to have spent her early months in her mother's household before being handed over to Alexander, 7th Lord Livingston and his wife Helen, Lady Livingstone. They took their young charge to Linlithgow Palace where they would raise Princess Elizabeth away from the royal court. Although Anna saw her daughter frequently given Lady Livingstone was a member of the queen's household it must have been difficult to hand over her baby daughter. Prince Henry never met his sister as a baby and his life carried on as normal regardless of the royal birth.

The Livingstons would take care of Elizabeth up to the age of 6 when her mother departed for England, during that time James created Alexander the 1st Earl of Linlithgow and despite his clear loyalty to the crown questions were raised over the appointment of Lady Livingston given the fact she was openly Catholic. James would visit Elizabeth and her younger sister Margaret often and whilst Elizabeth thrived under the care of the Livingston, sadly Margaret did not. She had been born at Dalkeith Castle on 24 December 1598 and joined her elder sister at Linlithgow after her baptism. Sadly, by March 1600, the little princess had contracted an unknown illness and died shortly after, her little body was transported from Linlithgow to Holyrood for burial. As far as Elizabeth was concerned, as she grew older it became more and more apparent that she was going to be an important asset to Scotland, a bonny princess that could be married off for political gain. At around the age of 7, rumours began to circulate that she was to marry Filippo Emmanuel, Prince of Savoy but nothing came of the match. When James took the English throne in 1603 she became a princess of England and all of a sudden the stakes were much higher and James could look for a more lucrative match.

A further son was born to Anna and James at Dunfermline Palace on 19 November 1600, he was named Charles but was considered a sickly child and was to be raised at Dunfermline by Alexander Seton, Lord Fyvie who formed part of Anna's household. Due to his apparent sickness,

Charles was taken to Holyrood to be baptised by David Lindsay, after the ceremony he was returned to the nursery at Dunfermline. The birth and loss of their children brought James and Anna closer together, theirs may not have been a great love story but a mutual and respectful relationship developed over time. Both shared the vision of a successful monarchy, a monarchy that was to stretch south of the border to England and when news reached James that Elizabeth I was dead and he was now King of England, their dream was realised.

Part II

1603–1613

By the will of King Henry VIII, James VI of Scotland should never have inherited the throne of England because he decided, for reasons unknown to us, to discount the Scottish decedents of his elder sister Margaret, wife of James V. We know that Henry was closer to his younger sister Mary and she had married Charles Brandon, Duke of Suffolk in 1515, and had three surviving daughters by him including Frances, the mother of Lady Jane Grey.

James had long awaited to be declared King of England because that stronger, wealthier and more powerful neighbour to the south was a coveted prize. This would be a seismic event that altered the fortunes of James and his young family, let alone the people of England and Scotland.

Elizabeth I, Queen of England died on 24 March 1603 at Richmond Palace in Surrey. Her body lay in state at Richmond before being conveyed down the River Thames to Whitehall for burial at Westminster. Whilst her body lay in the palace chapel, plans were quickly being arranged for her successor to make haste to London to claim the throne. Lady Scrope, a close confidant of Elizabeth, removed a sapphire ring from the queen's finger and dropped it from a window to an already mounted Robert Carey below. Carey was a cousin of Elizabeth and the task of riding north had fallen to him. He set off for Scotland determined to reach Edinburgh before anyone else could break the news of his queen's death. In the early hours of 26 March 1603, Robert Carey arrived at Holyrood, after galloping from London, stopping only to change horses. When he arrived, the palace was quiet but he managed to gain access and urge the footman to wake his king. James was roused immediately and Carey handed to him the blue sapphire ring that told the Scottish king Elizabeth was dead and he was now king of England. Robert Carey was the first person to greet him as thus. In the morning of the 24 March King James VI of Scotland was proclaimed King James I of England from the gates of Whitehall and as the news spread across London it was met by a subdued crowd. This was not because they didn't want James as their king, he was always the favourite to succeed, but because they were mourning the loss of their queen who had ruled for nearly 45 years. However, by the evening the bonfires were lit and the bells were tolling as the dawn of a new era began.

As soon as the news of James's accession broke preparations began for his departure south and it was clear he would not rest until he sat upon the English throne with the crown atop his head. On 2 April both the king and queen attended a service of thanksgiving at St Giles Cathedral in Edinburgh. James gave a speech in which he promised to visit every three years, but he returned only once over the course of the next twenty-two years. On the 5 April James left Edinburgh and headed for England, before he left, he wrote to his son and heir Prince Henry and told him he had no time to visit but that he was to remain well behaved for Lady Mar. The decision to travel alone to England and leave his family north of the border has never really been explained. One reason could have been for safety concerns, no one really knew how James was going to be received, especially in the north of England and he wouldn't have wanted to subject his wife and children to potential scenes of unrest. On the other hand, it has been suggested Anna could not enter England until her English ladies had completed their period of mourning for Elizabeth, either way, James made is progress alone. No sooner had James left Scotland, Anna travelled to Stirling to reclaim her son. The earl of Mar had to leave and accompany James to England given his previous experience with the English court so it was left to Lady Mar to stand firm and remind the Queen of James's strict instructions that the young prince was to stay in their care until he reached the age of 18, a rule James did not think to change before leaving for England. Anna was pregnant at the time and even though they initially denied her access to the castle they soon relented given her condition. Once inside the royal quarters she refused point blank to leave without her son and it fell to Lord Fyvie to try and persuade her to travel to England without her precious prince. She was so angry that in a rage she beat herself hard on the stomach until blood began to trickle down her legs. The councillors were so panicked they brought Henry to see his mother. Sadly, it was not enough to save the unborn child, Anna miscarried a baby boy and for a time there was genuine fear for the queen's life. She lay still and silent for days, Fyvie wrote to James to advise him what had happened and asked what they ought to do. James sent the ever-reliable Earl of Mar home to deal with the situation, however, he was the last person Anna would have wanted near her. Over the next few days, Anna began to regain her strength but the divide between Mar and his supporters and the queen and hers grew wider. Anna still refused to leave Stirling without her son and she had her husband right where she wanted him. She refused to leave the country that her children inhabited, James on the other hand wanted, and needed, his wife and children beside him in London in a show of Stuart solidarity. In the end, Anna was triumphant and left Stirling Castle on 23 May with her son beside her, the 6-year-old Princess Elizabeth joined them in Edinburgh just a few days later marking the first time the siblings had met. It didn't take long for an everlasting bond to form between them with Prince Henry declaring he loved his little sister very much. On 11 June Queen Anna, Prince Henry Frederick and Princess Elizabeth left Scotland and headed for London, Prince Charles, aged 3, was considered too small and sickly to travel such a distance and was left in Scotland where he was to receive intensive medical treatment. He became the royal family's only representative left in Scotland and there were possible rumours that he was to stay in Scotland as it's prince and rule on behalf of his father. That plan never came to fruition and Charles would join the family in London a year later.

Once the royal party had left Berwick in the middle of June, they headed south, tracking the route James had taken just weeks earlier. They stayed for four days at York as the guests of Thomas Cecil, Lord Burghley and from there travelled south to Worksop where they rested for three days as the guests of Gilbert Talbot, the 7th Earl of Shrewsbury. It was at Worksop Manor that James had stayed and enjoyed the hunt weeks before his family arrived. It was here that Elizabeth parted ways with her mother and brother and travelled onto Coombe Abbey, a future home of the princess, whilst the rest of the travelling party visited Market Harborough and Althorp. The family were reunited at Windsor Castle by mid-July.

When James became King of England Princess Elizabeth's status changed dramatically and with Prince Charles left behind in Scotland, she was considered second in line to the throne. Her new role as a Princess of England meant things had to change, her expenses rose as it became important for her to be perceived as a grand royal princess. An English princess was a much grander prize on the marriage market than a Scottish one and proposals came in thick and fast for Elizabeth's hand in marriage. There was a suggestion of a potential marriage to the Dauphin of France. The French Ambassador, Comte de Beaumont, was told that Elizabeth had become infatuated with the Dauphin's miniature portrait and he was just as flattering in his description of the young princess reporting back to France she was 'very well bred and handsome enough, rather tall for her age, and her disposition very gentle'. I find it interesting that she is described as tall, a trait she must have inherited from her paternal grandmother and one-time queen of France, Mary, Queen of Scots. Other than having her looks to recommend her, Elizabeth excelled at hunting, which she had done from a young age and was fluent in Italian by the age of 14.

It was a time of great joy in England as the country had not had royal children in the nursery since the birth of Edward VI in 1537 and James knew his children were a valuable asset to have. So, to celebrate this, he ordered both Elizabeth and Henry were to have their portraits painted by court artist Robert Peake. The princess is dressed in a white satin gown and in her left hand she is holding a fan which displays her age, 7, on the handle whilst the year, 1603, is inscribed into the bridge in the background (see image one). This was certainly a portrait to be used in the marriage market as you can see, she is in the full bloom of youth, her skin is pale and her face pretty, like her grandmother Mary, Queen of Scots, Elizabeth would grow into a tall, beautiful woman who had confidence and personality. Unfortunately, she would also match her grandmother in heartbreak too, but more on that later.

Elizabeth settled into English court life fairly quickly alongside her devoted elder brother Prince Henry Frederick. The two of them had formed a close relationship and were sent to live at Oatlands, a palace built by Henry VIII which sat nestled alongside the River Thames in Surrey. It would later belong to their mother and it became a favourite residence of hers but in 1603 it became the court of the royal children. Well known for its well-stocked deer park, Henry and Elizabeth spent much of their time hunting together and learning. She taught him Italian in exchange for him teaching her Latin. For the time, it was considered unusual for the royal children to be housed together, especially the two eldest but an outbreak of the plague forced James to send both his children to the safety of Winchester. As the heir, Henry would later return to London, making St James's Palace his premier residence, being in close proximity to his father would provide him with the opportunity to learn the art of kingship. Meanwhile, in October 1603 an order was issued that passed the care of Princess Elizabeth to Lord and Lady Harington of Coombe Abbey. The separation of the siblings was heart breaking for both of them. Anna would most likely not have involved herself too much in her son's upbringing but her daughter's education and well-being was her domain and one of the first things the queen did when she arrived in England was appoint the Dowager Countess of Kildare as Elizabeth's governess. Frances Fitzgerald was the daughter of Charles Howard, 1st Earl of Nottingham and her appointment as Elizabeth's governess was controversial and attempts were made to discredit her. The Earl of Northampton had tried to sully her name by accusing her of being involved in correspondence between English courtiers and James before he had succeeded to the throne. Nonetheless, she arrived at Windsor alongside Elizabeth in a litter pulled by thirty horses. But she was to lose her position in September 1603 when her husband was named in a catholic plot to take the king's life and place Elizabeth on the throne of England.

It didn't take long for the conspiracies to begin. The first to be foiled was a plot to kidnap and assassinate the entire royal family and replace

James with his cousin Arbella Stuart. Arbella was the only child of Charles Stuart, James's uncle, and Elizabeth Cavendish, daughter of the redoubtable Bess of Hardwick. Her claim to the throne was given serious consideration with some even seeing her as a more natural successor to Elizabeth I given she was born in England. Crucially, this plot was backed by Elizabethan statesman and explorer Sir Walter Raleigh with the aim of it being to bring a much greater tolerance for Catholics. Henry Brooke, 11th Baron Cobham had written to Arbella with details of the plot but they misjudged what her reaction would be and she passed the letter directly to the Secretary of State, Robert Cecil. Arbella was either completely taken aback by the suggestion in the letter or she was being very astute knowing that at some point the plot would fail, either way, the plot was exposed. Cobham was Cecil's brother-in-law and husband of Lady Kildare, who despite the link to the plot remained in her post as Elizabeth's governess. James had known Lady Kildare for many years and she had shown her loyalty to him when she performed the role of his spy at the court of Elizabeth I. But her ongoing support of her husband forced James to appoint the Haringtons as Elizabeth's guardians, relieving Lady Kildare of her duties.

Cobham and Raleigh were arrested and imprisoned but when they came to trial it appeared the evidence was flawed and the pair remained imprisoned at the Tower of London. Raleigh was released in 1616 and permitted to go on an expedition to find El Dorado, a trip that was sanctioned by James on the understanding he agreed not to interfere in any Spanish interests. James was keen to avoid any further costly conflict with the Spanish and he didn't want Raleigh jeopardising that. Despite agreeing, Raleigh violated the terms of this agreement and upon his return to England, the Spanish ambassador demanded his arrest and execution. James agreed and Sir Walter Raleigh was beheaded in the Old Palace Yard at Westminster on 29 October 1618, he was 65 years old. He had been an influential figure throughout the Elizabethan era and a favourite of Elizabeth I's but James had no such loyalty. Lord Cobham was released from the Tower in 1618 but died shortly after.

By December 1603, Elizabeth and Henry Frederick were separated, which they both protested against. Henry returned to London and Elizabeth went to Coombe Abbey in the midlands to begin her formal education. She was taught to dance by Francis Cardell, the son of Elizabeth I's tutor. The link to the old queen didn't stop there as the young Elizabeth's music teacher John Bull also taught her elder namesake. She was taught writing by Frenchman Jean de Beau-Chesne, a writer that Elizabeth I had admired. It was important to James that his daughter be well taught in languages, he perhaps envisaged a diplomatic future for her, or a foreign marriage, thankfully she excelled at learning. The French ambassador, Antoine Lefevre, commented that Elizabeth's grasp of French was excellent and even better than that of Prince Henry. By the age of 7, Elizabeth could write letters in French and by 13, in Italian, we can assume she was also fluent in speaking these languages. The parallels between the Princess and the Tudor Queen are striking and it has been suggested the younger Elizabeth was given access to Elizabeth I's papers which lent themselves to her copying the queen's signature. It is clear the princess had an admiration for the queen and she was happy to embrace the similarities between the two.

The education Elizabeth received under the Haringtons was fit for a queen; their family library was extensive and no doubt the princess was encouraged to read from it as often as she pleased. The time she spent with the Haringtons, and the level of education they provided for her, would later influence how she educated her own children, especially her daughters. Lord Harington proved to be a major influence over his young charge, especially her religious ideals, making him largely responsible for her staunch protestant beliefs.

But it wasn't just her education that flourished, her household also began to grow in numbers which also meant, so did her expenses but Elizabeth was generous in nature and ensured her staff were well paid. She made sure she was dressed how a princess ought to have been, spending vast sums on fine fabrics, pearls and feathers to adorn her luxurious gowns which she further accessorised with gloves, silk stockings and shoes. It seems she had inherited her parents love of fine things and of amassing huge debts. It appeared Elizabeth had created her own mini court that she sat at the centre of. Her life seemed idyllic and somewhat mystical, but that was to shatter in 1605 when the life of her father came under serious threat.

Robert Catesby was a well-born English Catholic who became disillusioned by James's lack of tolerance for Catholics which was something he had previously indicated he would support. Together, with a group of other like-minded men, a plot began to develop that became the biggest threat to the monarchy the country had ever seen. The group planned to blow up the king and his heir along with the government at the state opening of parliament on 5 November 1605, this became known as the Gunpowder Plot and is still remembered to this day. Once they had accomplished that, they were to place Elizabeth on the throne, marry her to a catholic and return the country back to Rome.

Catesby's mother, Anne Throckmorton, had an estate that lay just under twenty miles from Coombe Abbey meaning that when the time came, access to Elizabeth would be relatively easy. Along with others, Catesby went hunting but what they were actually doing was scoping out an opportunity to kidnap the princess. He arranged for all Lord Harington's horses to be stolen from his stables at Warwick Castle making an escape tricky. Thankfully, Harington sensed something dangerous was coming and wrote to the Earl of Salisbury asking him to bring his fears to the attention of the king. Harington was thinking on his feet and decided to remove Elizabeth from the remote Coombe Abbey and transfer her to the safety of Coventry. But no royal help was coming as the message never got through, Salisbury wrongly assumed Harington was complaining about the theft of his horses and failed to read the letter thoroughly. Thankfully, the city of Coventry was ready to defend its princess, as she was safely ensconced behind its defensive walls the people were ready and willing to come out and fight any would-be attacker. Harington went out to recruit men and arms in case they were needed, Elizabeth was well protected thanks to the quick thinking of her guardian and she wrote to her brother Henry to advise him she was safe and awaited further news. Little did they know in Coventry that in London the plot to blow up

Parliament had been foiled. If it had been successful it would have wiped out the king, his heir and his government, the establishment would have been obliterated in one explosion.

A Yorkshire man by the name of Guy Fawkes was caught red-handed by the barrels of gunpowder that had been strategically placed in a cellar under the houses of Parliament. When he was questioned and later tortured he confessed the plan was to place the 9-year-old Elizabeth on the throne, marry her to a catholic and return England to Catholicism. Given her age, a regent would have been needed to rule and whilst there was no evidence to prove it, it was widely assumed the catholic Henry Percy, 9th Earl of Northumberland was the preferred option. The plan was to leave the 5-year-old Prince Charles alone given he was too well protected in London, they reckoned he could be dealt with a later date and given his well-publicised health issues no one expected him to live long anyway.

The Catholic plotters may well have planned to place Elizabeth on the throne as a puppet queen but even at her young age she was her own person who knew her own mind with an independent spirit. Her response when she heard the news from London was:

> 'What a Queen should I have been by this means? I had rather have been with my royal father in the Parliament House, than wear his crown on such a condition.'

The Gunpowder Plot highlighted just how vulnerable James's grasp on the crown was, (even to this day, a sweep of the cellars under the Houses of Parliament is done and a Member of Parliament is taken hostage for the duration of the State opening of Parliament in order to ensure the safety of the monarch), he needed to make serious changes if he was going to sit easy on his throne. Firstly, he decided that Elizabeth was too far from the court in London and whilst he recognised the need to keep his children apart for safety reasons, it now became clear that Coombe Abbey was no longer suitable. In 1606, the decision was made to move Elizabeth to Kew, which sat on the south bank of the River Thames in

Surrey, making it easier for her to visit court and her family. No doubt this thrilled her as it meant she was close to her beloved elder brother Henry and even though they were not back to sharing a household they were close enough to be able to pay each other visits. He made expensive gifts to his sister including new gowns and horses and Elizabeth was more than happy to repay the privilege. It was a tender relationship that Harington encouraged as it meant Elizabeth was happy and content.

As they grew older, Elizabeth and Henry grew closer, they would often spend time with each enjoying the hunt and riding out together but it was inevitable things would change as their lives were on different paths. Henry was the future King of England, Scotland and Ireland whereas Elizabeth would be expected to marry and leave court and maybe even the country. When James became King of England in 1603 it was only natural his children would be highly coveted in the marriage market across Europe. Many suggestions were made for Elizabeth including Henry Howard, 1st Earl of Northampton and the Prince of Piedmont, Filippo Emmanual but all were declined. King Karl IX nominated his son and heir Gustavus Adolphus as a potential bridegroom but his ongoing dispute with Denmark meant that match was unlikely. There were even talks of double marriage proposals. The Prince of Piedmont was once again put forward by his father (this was Victor Amadeus, his elder brother Filippo Emmanual died of smallpox in 1605) but this time the hand of his daughter Maria was also put forward as a potential bride for Henry Frederick. The issue for James was that Savoy held much less power than Spain and France and whilst the dukedom held a strategic power it could be exploited by a much bigger force.

When Philip III of Spain's wife, Margaret of Austria, died in 1611 rumours began to spread that he wanted Elizabeth as his new bride despite the age gap being over twenty years. This was a proposal that caused concern at the Stuart court given Spain's Catholicism whereas Queen Anna on the other hand favoured the match given her family links with the Habsburgs. Again, a double proposal was offered with Philip's eldest daughter Anne being put forward as a potential bride for Prince Henry. A double marriage with Spain was a very attractive offer, Spain was a European powerhouse and ties with them would be advantageous but James chose to decline both offers, after all, would it have been wise to put all his eggs in the Spanish basket? The past showed James that marriage alliances could be broken and peace made elsewhere so it would have been too much of a risk to fully align himself with one country. He even shut down talks over a potential marriage with King Louis XIII of France upon the advice of his ministers. A match that might have interested the queen was one with her nephew Frederick Ulrich, the future Duke of Brunswick-Lüneburg. He travelled to the English court in the hope of securing Elizabeth's hand but sadly he was declined as he was not considered a grand enough match.

James looked towards protestant Europe; it was suggested that if he married his daughter to a Protestant then he could marry his son to a Catholic and when in 1610 Frederick IV, Elector of Palatine died his 14-year-old son Frederick became the new Calvinist Elector and needed a wife. Frederick had previously been discussed as being a potential suitor but was dismissed, however, now he was the Elector Palatinate of the Rhine, one of the most powerful Electors in the Holy Roman Empire, he all of a sudden became a person of interest. Intense negotiations took place and on 26 May 1612, a marriage contract between Frederick V and Princess Elizabeth was signed, much to the queens annoyance. Frederick, who was due to assume his titles when he came of age at 18, and Elizabeth began exchanging letters in French, he sent his bride a piece of jewellery to which Elizabeth told her groom she would wear it 'because I am commanded to so by the king'. Both knew their duty was to marry for the better of their nation and Elizabeth was under no illusions this was anything but a political union, if it turned out to be a love match then that was a bonus.

Frederick, who was childlike in his appearance, was to make the journey to London to claim his bride and in readiness, Elizabeth's household moved from Kew to Whitehall where she was to become a permanent member of the court. The movement of any royal household was no easy task, all the people, animals and Elizabeth's personal belongings had to be packed up and moved downstream and her servants would have to up their standards and learn the court rules. Frederick left his home in Heidelberg on 17 September 1612 and travelled via Cologne and the Dutch Republic, where he would finally set sail for England in a fleet of eight ships. Unfortunately, his first attempt to sail saw his flotilla beaten back by heavy wind and storms. In a situation not too dissimilar to James and Anna's courtship, James sent three English ships to Maassluis to bring Frederick to England, arriving at Gravesend on the evening of 26 October.

James planned for Frederick to be met by the court and 500 of London's wealthiest citizens as he approached the city. He sailed up the Thames accompanied by the Duke of Lennox alongside a flotilla of royal barges which carried large groups of noblemen. As he sailed upstream, Elizabeth sailed in the opposite direction, albeit with less fuss, to Whitehall. When Frederick was presented to the king and queen, James embraced him but Anna was much frostier giving him a hard stare as she raised her hand to be kissed. Anna was unhappy with her husband's choice of groom for their daughter; she labelled her 'Goodwife Palsgrave' whilst Elizabeth reportedly referred to her mother as the greatest papist queen in Christendom. Clearly there was no love lost between mother and daughter but Prince Henry gave his approval for the match and for Elizabeth, that was enough. When presented to his future wife, Frederick kissed the hem of Elizabeth's gown, marking their formal introduction.

This was to be no proxy wedding as James wanted to view Frederick in person before any marriage could take place. He would have been met with a serious young man but he was pleased with what he saw and Frederick quickly became a popular member of the English court. It appeared the young betrothed couple were more than satisfied with each other and they soon began to see each other in her apartments, away from her parents watchful eyes. They often dined together with Prince Henry at his residence St James's Palace, and it was clear to all that the young couple were becoming infatuated with each other creating a buzz of excitement around court, that was until Prince Henry fell fatally ill.

On 20 October after a heavy meal with Elizabeth and Frederick, Prince Henry decided to take a swim in the icy River Thames, something which he indulged in regularly. After complaining of feeling ill his physician

Dr John Hammond, provided the prince with an enema and laxatives before telling him to rest, unfortunately, Henry ignored this advice and carried on with his normal day, including playing sports. On 4 November, Henry attended a sermon looking 'pale and thin, his eyes hollow and dull' later that day whilst he was dining with his father he fainted and had to be carried to his bed. The queen appointed her own physician Theodore de Mayerne to take over the care of her son and after an initial examination diagnosed the prince with a tertian fever. No one seemed overly concerned as the family were prone to fits of fainting and illness but little did they realise, Henry would never leave his rooms again.

By the Wednesday, his bouts of diarrhoea had turned into daily fevers and his treatment was increased, all his court duties had to be cancelled, causing gossip to spread. His physicians started to bleed him, a common treatment for the day and initially it seemed to be working as he appeared to get a little stronger each day but in reality all it did was weaken him even further. He seemed to be progressing so well that his parents and Elizabeth believed he had overcome the worst and the court, which up to this point had been holding its breath, let out a huge sigh of relief. Sadly, they were wrong and on 12 November his condition deteriorated even further, he continued to be bled and rather bizarrely he had his head shaved in order for the doctor to apply a freshly killed pigeon to his scalp. The endless stream of bloodletting, medicines and enemas were of no use and it soon became clear that Prince Henry was dying. Henry Frederick, Prince of Wales died aged 18 years old on 6 November 1612 at St James's Palace, his dying words were 'Where is my dear sister?'. Elizabeth tried several times to gain access to her brother's rooms but was refused entry each time, she even donned various disguises to fool the doormen, but no one was taken in and she never saw her beloved elder brother again. The king and queen were naturally devastated by their son's death but it did little to reunite them, James headed to Theobalds with his latest favourite, the Earl of Rochester, whilst Anna locked herself away at Somerset House in London.

The people of England and Scotland openly mourned for their lost prince. Henry had been popular and his death threatened to plunge

England into another succession crisis just nine years after the last one. James and Anna of course had another son, Prince Charles but he had been weak and sickly from birth and at 12 years old still seemed frail. There was no realistic chance that Anna could conceive and give birth to another child so the hopes of a nation rested on Prince Charles.

Naturally, Elizabeth was devastated at the loss of her brother causing her to go two full days without eating, Queen Anna even feared for her daughter's life. Despite her grief, Elizabeth still had duties to perform as the court was plunged into mourning. Henry's body lay in state for four weeks at St James's Palace with the funeral taking place on 7 December 1612 at Westminster Abbey whilst other ceremonies were undertaken at Oxford, Cambridge and Bristol. Over 2000 people took place in the procession, which was led by Prince Charles, with many more lining the streets. James, Anna and Elizabeth did not attend as was custom of the day but Frederick and his entourage followed Prince Charles. The hearse carried a wooden effigy, made by Richard Norris, of Henry fully clothed in the robes he wore at his investiture as Prince of Wales in 1612. According to the Westminster Abbey website, the robes had been stolen by 1616 whilst his head had been removed by 1872. His body was finally laid to rest in the vault of his grandmother, Mary, Queen of Scots, in the Lady Chapel which had been built by his three-times great-grandfather Henry VII. Prince Henry was just 18 years old when he died and with him went the hopes of a nation. He brought so much optimism and positivity for a bright future, with his physique and enthusiasm he reminded many of the last great king the country had had, his namesake, Henry VIII. That now lay in tatters and the royal family had to somehow move forward and look to the future with Prince Charles as the heir to the three crowns.

Elizabeth's grief was clear for all to see and people gave her gifts in an attempt to cheer her mood, these included a horse and a pet dog from her father that had once belonged to Henry. She was also keen to preserve her brother's memory and legacy by supporting and encouraging authors who wrote pamphlets which celebrated the prince's life. But there is always the dark side of grief and Elizabeth's came out in her gambling addiction; she gambled with funds she did not have playing against courtiers at billiards on the outside enjoying herself whilst deep down the loss of her brother was agonising for her. As she battled with her grief her education had to continue. Her personal records show she was a keen reader owning a copy of Foxe's *Book of Martyrs* and other various historical titles that charted her ancestry. Learning would be something Elizabeth would turn to in her adult life she was always keen to expand her knowledge making her one of the most well-educated women of her age.

Prince Charles, Duke of York was now the heir to the throne and his ill health and frailty, which he had suffered from birth, meant uncertainty lay over the succession. Questions were beginning to be asked about whether Elizabeth ought to be allowed to leave the country as the wife of a foreign prince, or, whether she should perhaps stay in England as its heiress. Given Charles's weaknesses, many courtiers supported Elizabeth's claim to the throne which meant concerns over her security grew. Those concerns grew even stronger when rumours that Prince Henry had been poisoned began to circulate, even though there was no evidence to support this theory from his autopsy. Some even believed James himself had poisoned his son, although why he would remain a mystery. These were serious accusations and in order to protect herself, Elizabeth purchased Narwhal's tusk and blessed thistle that were supposed to detect poison in her food and drink.

Naturally, the wedding plans for Elizabeth and Frederick had to change. The marriage ceremony had originally been scheduled for 7 April 1613 and James had considered delaying it until at least May, although many members of his Privy Council felt it should be cancelled altogether given the princess's new elevated status. Some even thought she should be marrying elsewhere now she was one step closer to the throne but the original marriage agreement had been signed in May 1612 and as this was the official engagement announcement laying out the conditions by which Elizabeth would live by in Heidelberg to renege on this would have been frowned upon across Europe. In fact, the opposite had taken place and the document was amended on 27 November 1612, just eleven days after Henry's death, which urged for the marriage to take place as a matter of urgency and that the vows should be exchanged on 6 January. James clearly wanted his daughter married to halt speculation and to stop any dissenting voices from gaining any further traction. The ceremony took place at 10 am at the Banqueting House with the king and the greatest nobility in attendance. Elizabeth's wedding gown was made of black satin trimmed with silver lace and she wore a plume of white feathers in her hair. The right balance needed to be struck between the joy of the union and the grief the court was still experiencing. Frederick wore purple velvet with a lace of gold trim. Queen Anna did not attend her daughter's wedding due to illness; she had been away from court since Henry's death and was reported to have been suffering from a severe attack of gout. She was also not overly happy about the marriage and rueing a lucrative match with Spain which still clearly smarted with her. To celebrate afterwards, there were fireworks and mock sea battles that took place on the river.

On 14 February 1613, Elizabeth and Frederick publicly solemnised their wedding in the Royal Chapel at Whitehall. The ceremony had originally been scheduled to take place at Westminster Abbey but was considered inappropriate given its close proximity to Henry's newly occupied tomb. Elizabeth's gown was made of cloth of silver and was encrusted with pearls and her train took fourteen ladies to carry. On her head she wore a gold crown which allowed her hair, which was dressed with the finest pearls, to hang loosely down her back. Frederick wore a white satin suit with pearl and gold accessories and was accompanied by sixteen men, one for each of his years. The procession to the chapel began with Frederick and then came Elizabeth on the arm of her guardian Lord Harington with Lady Harington following the train carriers. Then came the daughters of the country's leading noblemen, and courtiers, followed by four Heralds-at-Arms. After them the Earls, Lords and Barons, the King of Heralds, the Lords of the Privy Council, four bishops, and four Sergeants of the mace. Following all of that came the king and queen, the Earl of Arundel carried James's sword of state before him whilst Anna was attended by her greatest ladies. James wore a black suit with a Spanish cape and was bedecked in fine jewels whilst Anna was dressed in white satin and diamonds. Following the ceremony Elizabeth changed her gown to one of gold and the whole court was treated to a performance of writer Thomas Champion's *The Lord's Masque* and *The Tempest* by William Shakespeare was a gift to the newlyweds and was performed fourteen times by the King's Men, the sets were designed by famed designer Inigo Jones. The wedding of his only daughter was an opportunity for James to show off his wealth. His queen was dazzling in diamonds but he ensured his daughter sparkled the brightest for her big day. The solemn ceremony was conducted by George Abbot, Archbishop of Canterbury. That evening the marriage was consummated and Elizabeth and Frederick began their married life together but the celebrations didn't end there, in the days that followed there were many masques and firework displays for the guests to enjoy. The total cost of the wedding came to £93,278 (approximately £12 million in today's money) and that amount does not include the price of the jewels. How James was going to pay for it was going to prove a struggle as the country was in financial difficulty. The city of Edinburgh had promised a dowry of £10,000 at the time of Elizabeth's birth and the sum of £20,500 was collected by a raise in taxes leaving the amount of £62, 778 needing to be found. The wedding added dramatically to the state deficit and the bills were still being settled in 1637 and well into the reign of Charles I!

Part III

1613–1621

Elizabeth was escorted to Heidelberg by Ludovick Stuart, 2nd Duke of Lennox, son of her father's one-time favourite, who had been the one to escort her from Scotland just ten years earlier, and he was by her side once again for the next great journey of her life. The journey began with Elizabeth and Frederick being joined by her family as they sailed down the Thames from Whitehall to Greenwich and from there they travelled on to Rochester in Kent at which point James and Anna took leave of their daughter. When a daughter married abroad it was more often than not that you would never see each other again, travel in the seventeenth century took time, especially across countries and as Elizabeth bid her parents farewell she must have known she would never see either of them again. Prince Charles accompanied his sister and brother-in-law to Canterbury to attend several civic functions before returning to Windsor. On 5 May 1613, Princess Elizabeth sailed from English shores at Margate alongside her new husband aboard the *Prince Royal*. They were greeted at Ostend, in modern day Belgium, by Maurice of Nassau, his half-brother Frederick Henry and brother-in-law the catholic Prince of Portugal, Manuel. Everyone was convinced to join the newlyweds on aboard the *Prince Royal* to dine that evening.

An entourage of 373 accompanied Elizabeth and on 9 May they reached Flushing, from there, Frederick rode on to The Hague on business with the Protestant Union. Elizabeth was taken to the city Middelburg, a province in the Dutch Republic where she was hosted by Maurice who entertained his royal guest lavishly, Elizabeth enjoyed the finest food and drink he had to offer. From Middelburg, Elizabeth then travelled to the small town of Veere and it was from here she bid goodbye to her English escort. As they turned back towards England Elizabeth continued on to Willemstad, Dordrecht, Rotterdam and Delft before reuniting with Frederick at The Hague where they spent three days together. Frederick went on ahead to Heidelberg to make the necessary preparations for Elizabeth's arrival, in the meantime she continued on to Leiden, Haarlem, Amsterdam, Utrecht, Rhenen and Arnhem where she had the opportunity to stay with relatives of her mother. Her progress then continued to Nijmegen and Zaltbommel finally leaving the United Provinces on 30 May. The United Provinces, otherwise known as the Dutch Republic, came into existence in January 1579 with the Union of Utrecht. It was formed of seven provinces who came together to form an alliance against the harsh Spanish rule under Philip II of Spain. There was a good reason for Elizabeth's extended journey through the republic and that was to promote the alliance between England and the Protestant Union. The Protestant Union had been formed in 1608 and was a military alliance amongst the German States as protection against the increasing power of the Roman Catholic states under the Counter Reformation that had taken hold throughout the Holy Roman Empire. When the Diet (Reichstag) of the Holy Roman Empire met the Catholic Princes they made it clear they wanted the return of all confiscated church land and goods that had been seized during the Protestant Reformation. Six of the Protestant Princes, including Frederick's father, Frederick IV, Elector Palatine of the Rhine, broke away from the Diet to form the alliance that would stand for ten years. Within that ten-year period, they all pledged military support to each other should they be attacked. Alongside Frederick IV were the Dukes of Neuburg and Württemberg and the Margraves of Ansbach, Baden-Durlach and Kulmbach. Beside the Protestant Union stood the Dutch Republic, Sweden and England who also pledged military backing should it be needed. James had been keen on a Protestant marriage for Elizabeth and now her husband was the head of the Protestant Union it gave him great access to religious powers on the continent. In response to the Union, the Catholic Princes formed the Catholic League under the guidance and leadership of Duke Maximilian I of Bavaria. The Union will play a vital role in Frederick and Elizabeth's lives but long before that she had time to enjoy her early married life.

Along their travels, Elizabeth and Frederick received many gifts including a set of six tapestries depicting the story of Diana from a workshop in Delft. This was a gift that Elizabeth treasured more than most and one she took with her whenever she moved between residences. On the final leg of her journey, Elizabeth travelled through Cologne and onto her new home at Heidelberg arriving on 17 June 1613. Located on the banks of the River Neckar on the eastern side of the Upper Rhine Plain, the town of Heidelberg sits nestled between the Oden Forest and the Little Oden Forest. At the time Elizabeth reached her new home it was already well-established as a seat of learning with the university being founded in 1386, making it Germany's oldest university.

When she reached Heidelberg, Elizabeth was greeted by 'A 1000 Horses (all Gentlemen of the Country) who were very richly attired and bravely furnished with Armour' they then proceeded to welcome their new princess with a 25-round gun salute. With Fredrick absent, Elizabeth was welcomed into the hillside castle by her mother-in-law Louise Juliana of Orange-Nassau who was the half-sister of Maurice and Frederick Henry. Other noble ladies made up the welcoming party and they were all treated to spectacular pageants and tournaments which no doubt made Elizabeth feel at home given her love for performance. Having not seen Frederick since 18 May, she was keen to be reunited with her husband and she didn't have to wait too long as he arrived shortly after her welcoming party. The probable reason for his absence was to give Elizabeth centre stage and allow her the opportunity to see her new home without his influence. Not long after her arrival, Frederick wrote to James to confirm Elizabeth had arrived safely and the 'transaction' was now complete making the marriage sound more like a business deal than a happy match made in love. But a happy match it turned out to be and news quickly spread that Elizabeth was pregnant with her first child. This was not to say Elizabeth's arrival had been smooth, and soon arguments arose over who took precedence over who. Louise Juliana expected to take precedence over her daughter-in-law, but Elizabeth was a royal princess and the wife of the Elector so naturally she felt she had precedence as first lady of the land. This issue would be a constant headache for Frederick as his wife was a lady who knew her worth and wasn't afraid to speak out if she felt she was being slighted.

The Heidelberg court was as cosmopolitan as any other across Europe but when Elizabeth arrived with her blended court of English and Scottish lords and ladies they had to find a way to try and mix with German customs. Even Frederick had to adapt to his German court as he had primarily been brought up in France by his uncle the Duke of Bouillon and had developed their customs. But he quickly learnt that in order to have harmony at his court he had to keep his French flair in check and his wife happy. Until Frederick came of age the Duke of Zweibrücken-Veldenz governed the Palatinate along with the Dowager Electress and neither was willing to allow Elizabeth to reside at their courts. Heidelberg had four households at loggerheads with each other; each believing they should defer to the other. Elizabeth may have been the newcomer but as a princess of royal blood, she assumed (and so did James) that she held precedence over everyone, including her husband given he had not yet reached his majority. One solution was that Elizabeth should show deference to her husband but then she should take precedence over everyone else, both inside and outside of the castle, but this just caused even more conflict. The argument rumbled on.

There were genuine concerns amongst Elizabeth's nobles that the overseeing of her marriage settlement would take much longer than a month by which time many of those who had accompanied her would have to leave to return home to England and thereby leaving Elizabeth alone at the centre of a bickering court. Those that did remain refused to mix with the Germans or blend quietly into the background, the men in her household were Scottish whilst the majority of the women were English, this would have been because her father the King would have selected the male members of her household whilst her mother would have taken charge of appointing her ladies-in-waiting and they tended to be the daughters of the queen's ladies. James's decision to exclude English men from her household did not go down too well and the Germans weren't keen either as they soon had issues with the Scots too.

Elizabeth's new Master of the Household was Sir James Sandilands whilst her new Master of the Horse was a chap called Sir Andrew Keith. Both proved to be unpopular choices at court and with Elizabeth. Sandilands had replaced her loyal guardian Lord Harington and so was at an instant disadvantage but trouble followed him around. He even challenged German courtier Hans Schönberg, Master of the House, to a dual but was thankfully talked out of it. Keith didn't seem to learn from his countryman's behaviour and challenged one of Harington's servants to a dual, this finally gave Elizabeth the opportunity she had been waiting for to act and she immediately had Keith imprisoned. She had control over who was dismissed from her household but James and Anna had the final say over who she employed so as not to interfere with Frederick's household although it was probably so they could spy on their daughter and keep abreast of happenings in Europe. One thing James was adamant on at the time of the marriage negotiations was that Elizabeth and her household were to be given religious autonomy over Frederick's. As part of the marriage agreement, she was allowed to have her own chaplains to accompany her to Heidelberg and she chose Dr Scapman and Dr Twyst. She was to be able to worship as per the rites of the Church of England, she may have been a Protestant like her husband but she followed the rule and guidance of her mother church back home in England. To be able to accomplish this she was to be given her own private chapel making her the first Electress to have this privilege. Frederick never seemed to quibble over his father-in-law's demands for his daughter so we must assume that he was happy to oblige.

Heartbreaking news was to arrive in Heidelberg for Elizabeth, whilst on his way home to England to discuss the marriage settlement, Lord Harington died from a fever whilst at Worms, a town just 23 miles from Heidelberg. He was travelling to England in 1613 to speak with James about the finer points of the marriage settlement that had not yet been actioned. According to the agreement, Frederick was to assign a palace and town at Frankenthal to Elizabeth but those plans had yet to materialise. Along with Harington's death went the plans to discuss the issue with James giving Frederick and his court the opportunity to stall a little longer. We have no record of Elizabeth's feelings over the death of Harington; he had been the man who played the role of father figure to her for much of her young adult life. He had protected her as a child and advised her as an adult but records indicate she keeps silent during times of grief and so we have no letters written by her from this time. Harington left a wife and three children and a debt so large the family seat at Exton Hall in the county of Rutland had to be sold to pay off his creditors. No doubt much of this debt arose from the expenses he incurred whilst looking after Elizabeth as he got very little financial assistance from the crown.

Elizabeth was never completely satisfied with the castle at Heidelberg, and even though Frederick finally signed over the Palace at Frankenthal to his wife, it was not up to the standards Elizabeth was used to, but it would become an important place for her over the coming months and years. To make his wife more comfortable at Heidelberg, Frederick created a wing in the 'English Style' and laid out formal gardens. He wanted a palace fit for a princess but his family seat had no free space to allow for any further construction work, so, he designed the new wing that was to be built alongside the north wall so it actually sat outside the castle grounds. The structure that he built was a large four-sided building with the facades supporting large windows that would have let in the maximum amount of light. On the west side was the 'Thick Tower' which had been built in 1533, but in order to make the castle feel less like a defensive castle and more like a luxury palace, he added a room atop the tower which had sixteen corners and large windows. These would offer wrap around views of the surrounding town and countryside and was used as a dining room to entertain guests. The gardens were laid out between 1616 and 1619 and had features such as grottoes, raised ornate flower beds which were all set out across magnificent terraces. But all this work took time and Elizabeth remained at odds with the dramatic mountainside residence of her husband.

She may not have liked the castle, but life in Heidelberg was not all bad as Elizabeth enjoyed the hunt and in particular the hunting lodge at Beuheim which lay on her lands in the district of Germersheim, just under 20 miles from Heidelberg. Like her father, Elizabeth excelled at hunting and she impressed many with her riding skills and fearless and vigorous energy. She shot exceptionally well and even remained in the saddle when pregnant, although none dared tell her to stop and consider the health of her unborn child. She was self-assured, confident and a free spirit which many felt gave her a masculine air but to Elizabeth, the opportunity to hunt gave her a sense of freedom she could not achieve behind the walls of Heidelberg Castle.

The households of Elizabeth and Frederick had been run as two separate entities, but Elizabeth's pregnancy allowed Frederick's Hofmeister, Hans Meinhard von Schönberg, to interfere. In his mind, as she was carrying the heir to the Palatine House he felt he had the right to step in and meddle. He even went to England to update the king personally on Elizabeth's condition and on his plans for Heidelberg, all of which pleased James, how Elizabeth felt about his interference we do not know.

Joy came to Heidelberg when Elizabeth gave birth to a son on 1 January 1614, he was named Prince Frederick Henry in honour of his father and late uncle. He had a dark complexion and a full head of dark hair, a common Stuart trait that pleased James immensely. Schönberg had just left London when he heard the good news making him promptly turn around and head back to London so keen as he was to report the news to the new grandparents in person. The birth of Frederick Henry cemented the Stuart dynasty even further as he was potentially the heir to the thrones of England, Scotland and Ireland as well as being his father's heir in the Palatinate. Elizabeth also gained financially with the birth of her son when her father settled on her an annual payment for life of 12,000 crowns, to his grandson he sent a payment of 25,000 crowns, plate and jewels. In parliament, he declared that baby Frederick Henry was a prince born of English and Scottish blood and that he would be raised a true Protestant. The young prince was baptised with James as godfather, although Frederick's chief advisor, Prince Christian of Anhalt, stood as proxy along with 300 knights. The other godfather was the Prince and Stadholder Maurice, although his younger brother was sent in his place as proxy, there is no record of who stood as his godmother although given his high status we can assume it was a lady of great nobility.

When Schönberg returned home he had brought with him James's authority to take full control of Elizabeth's household away from Sandilands. She would also now receive £10,000 a year to safeguard her should she ever be made a widow and along with this came a quarterly payment of £51,500 which was backdated to the time of her wedding. The two households were now united and Frederick was to foot the wage bill for all forty-nine members of his wife's household. Unfortunately for him, Elizabeth was just like her father and ran up huge debts and even with a man like Schönberg around to guide her she spent way beyond her means. To get a handle on her spending, Schönberg insisted on authorising every payment made for the household, reluctantly she agreed but quickly learnt that Schönberg's interference would not end with her finances. He went as far as advising her how to keep her servants in line but some of his advice she welcomed and took on board and would later adopt when setting up her children's households. Over time, Elizabeth and Schönberg built up a friendly and respectful relationship and she would admit to having been lost without him by her side, he seemed to fill the void that Harington had left.

Just four weeks after the birth of her son, Elizabeth wrote to her father to update him on the Jülich-Berg and Cleves affair which was beginning to simmer. It all centred around a battle for succession in which the Catholics were threatening war against the Protestant Union. James requested Frederick and Schönberg travel to Jülich to help settle the tensions there. It had been a source of tension for some years, in 1609 James had offered to mediate between the two warring factions, it seemed to be successful but it is to be noted that whilst James was willing to negotiate peace by talking, he was not willing to offer any military help. In 1614, tensions rose again and James was once again willing to mediate by sending Frederick and Schönberg to act on his behalf. As time went on, his enthusiasm seemed to wane and he claimed that England ought to help settle the matter with the Dutch and without Spanish interference. Peace talks were to resume in The Hague; James supported the idea that Jülich should be governed by a neutral prince and he even made suggestions as to who he felt could fulfil the role. Sadly, not all parties could agree that any one prince could be truly neutral and the plan failed. Unfortunately, war broke out again and the region remained at odds well into the eighteenth century. By October 1614, Elizabeth and Frederick were back at Heidelberg discussing whether or not to go to war with Spain over their reluctance to relinquish their occupied territory. Frederick, as the leader of the Protestant Union, wrote to James to tell him the Palatine did not have the resources to go to war, Elizabeth wrote separately to her father advising him she backed her husband in all things.

Elizabeth's Lady-in-Waiting and Schönberg's wife, Anna Dudley, died in December 1615 following the birth of their first child. The pair had secretly been in love before they left England but James had disapproved of the match following concerns from her father. Elizabeth however did not share her father's doubts and happily gave her approval for their marriage. There was also the German custom that the highest-ranking lady in the princesses household ought to marry the highest placed gentleman from the Prince's household. Schönberg was devastated at the loss of his wife. Elizabeth was at her friend's side as she breathed her last and while she grieved her loss deeply James and Anna saw it as an opportunity to establish a new woman in her place and to extend their influence in their daughter's household. Elizabeth urged caution as the Palatinate was not to everyone's taste and it could be a difficult place to live. In the end, her parents sent Genevan born Louise de Mayerne, sister of King James's physician, Sir Théodore Turquet de Mayerne. How much input Elizabeth had over this choice we do not know but she accepted Louise into her household and later brokered her marriage on 20 September 1620 to Frederick's Gentleman of the Bedchamber, Zacharie de Jaucourt. Following the death of Anne Dudley, Elizabeth began to feel homesick, Louise de Mayerne didn't fill the void Anne had left, only one woman could, Lady Harington, so she requested a visit from 'ma bonne mere'. Lady Harington, who along with her husband, had been nothing short of surrogate parents to Elizabeth. Lady Harington, who was in her sixties, also took some English-speaking servants with her as she knew the German ones did not meet Elizabeth's standards.

The issue of precedence blew up again in 1616 during a state visit to Stuttgart and the baptism of the third son of the Duke of Württemberg. It had been agreed that Elizabeth would take precedence over Frederick in public but his fellow princes told him that was not the right order of things in their country. Elizabeth may have been a royal princess but that was in England, not Germany. Knowing she wouldn't be happy, Frederick advised his wife that from that point on she was to defer to him in public. Elizabeth was enraged and sent Schönberg to see her father, he was to explain that whilst at Heidelberg, Frederick had seemed happy for her to take precedence in public, but now she was expected to come after him. Rather surprisingly James agreed that Elizabeth should defer to her husband on some matters but that was standard practise for the time, it didn't matter if you were a queen and he a commoner, the second you married you became your husbands property. But publicly, when it came to rank, that was a whole other matter. For James, precedence was everything, she was the daughter of a king and he wrote to Elizabeth to express how proud he was of her for not giving up her right to precedence. Frederick was just going to have to accept it and learn to live with it, for he knew when he married Elizabeth that she would come first in the order as it formed part of the marriage negotiations. This rumbling argument threatened to cause a big rift between Elizabeth and Frederick and seriously damage their marriage and when on their return from Stuttgart she immediately left Heidelberg for Friedrichsbhül to hunt, it looked like the rift had begun. Elizabeth stated she would refrain from making any public appearances with Frederick given the upset it causes, some would see this as petulance on her part but she was brought up to believe in the divine right of kings and as the daughter of a king in her mind she trumped and Elector.

Great news came on 1 January 1618, when Elizabeth gave birth to her second son Prince Charles Louis. The cannons were fired across Heidelberg in celebration of the safe delivery of a second Palatine prince.

As a celebratory gift, James sent his daughter two monkeys which it was hoped would ease her homesickness. These may seem like unusual gifts, but at the time they were the height of luxury, James was well known for his menagerie of exotic animals which he kept at the Tower of London. But she still longed for home and Frederick refused her permission to visit her family and before long she was pregnant again. Elizabeth gave birth to her first daughter on 5 January 1619, who they named Elisabeth. Despite being a mother of three Elizabeth still yearned for a visit home but little did she realise her life was about to change forever.

In 1617, Mattias, King of Bohemia and Holy Roman Emperor, turned 60 years old and named his nephew, Ferdinand, Archduke of Austria as his successor. Mattias had hoped Ferdinand would travel to Bohemia to rule alongside him so that when the time came he would be well prepared to take the reins leading to a smooth transition of power. Sadly, it did little but spark a rebellion, a rebellion that Frederick openly supported. The concerns were that the Catholic Ferdinand would persecute the Protestants and that they would lose much of their freedom. So, they opted to oppose every Catholic official that Mattias appointed, including Ferdinand. In order to keep a lid on things he sent his Grand Chamberlain Johann Albrecht I, Count of Solms-Braunfels to ensure the rebels did not compromise and make peace with Mattias. As the leader of Protestant Union, it fell to Frederick to assure its members that he would not allow any prince to come to Mattias's aid and he was even willing to use his own money, along with the Duke of Savoy, to pay for 4000 soldiers. The Bohemian state of Silesia also lent its support to Frederick by sending a further 3000 soldiers meaning they could match the mighty Habsburgs in terms of power. They were to lay siege to the city of Pilsen, which had long been loyal to Mattias so the Protestant army marched on the imperial capital Vienna.

In March 1619, Queen Anna died at Hampton Court aged 44. She had been suffering from dropsy (oedema) for about four years; James wrote to Elizabeth to advise her of her mother's death. Elizabeth's relationship with her mother was affectionate but distant, Anna never seemed to be overly close to her daughter but much of that could have been down to royal protocols of the day. As Elizabeth grew older the religious differences caused increased tension between the pair leading to a somewhat frostier relationship. There also seems to be a lack of correspondence between them, Elizabeth wrote frequently to her father and brother but much less to her mother but regardless of that, she mourned her deeply when she heard of her passing. Their relationship never saw a public rift but at the same time they didn't seem to enjoy a close-knit relationship but the physical distance between them would not have helped maintain a closer bond.

That March also saw the death of Mattias, the Holy Roman Emperor, which meant Ferdinand finally became King of Bohemia but he did not automatically take the title of Holy Roman Emperor, that would be decided later. Ferdinand was not a popular choice as king despite his insistence that he would abide by the Letter of Majesty, a document signed by Rudolf II, King of Bohemia (1576-1611), granting religious tolerance across the Bohemian kingdom. But it still wasn't enough to placate the Protestant princes, Ferdinand urged all parties to meet in Vienna for peace talks but the Estates of all Lands of the Bohemian Crown convened on 31 July to form a confederation, and on 22 August they voted to depose Ferdinand as king. Four days later the crown of Bohemia was offered to Frederick and envoys were dispatched to see if this would be a viable option for him. During the interim of there being no Emperor, Frederick, as Elector Palatine, along with the Elector of Saxony, were installed as imperial vicars, which meant in the absence of an emperor they were to assume that role as an interim measure. It was their responsibility to call the remaining five electors together to elect a new emperor. Given that was going to be a member of the Habsburg dynasty, it was assumed Ferdinand would fill the role. It was important to Frederick that the imperial crown be awarded by election rather than by hereditary means. But in order for the Bohemian states to remain powerful and the Protestant Union strong, they had to consider non-Habsburg applicants, men such as the King of Denmark, the Dukes of Savoy, Bavaria and the Elector of Saxony, although he stopped short at nominating himself. But Frederick knew if he opposed Ferdinand he would lose out and become an enemy of the powerful Habsburgs. Ferdinand of Austria was elected Holy Roman Emperor on 28 August 1619 and he was crowned in Frankfurt on 9 September.

Frederick seemed to be dragging his feet in making a decision regarding the crown. On paper he seemed an excellent choice, he was young, gave good counsel and was a competent leader of the Protestant Union, he was also the most powerful prince in the empire. Frederick was also well connected, his family ties included the Princes of Orange-Nassau, the Dukes of Bouillion and Bavaria and he boasted the King of England, Scotland and Ireland as his father-in-law which meant he could call on support from right across Europe should he need to. The Elector was also widely praised for his religious tolerance, he was well respected, well-liked and much admired. But for Frederick, he was unsure as to whether to accept the crown or not, he turned to Elizabeth for advice and she immediately wrote to her father and brother requesting their support in Bohemia. Unfortunately, her letters fail to tell us if she was asking James to urge her husband to take the crown or whether she should dissuade him. We know from later correspondence that James was against his son-in-law taking the crown in fact, he expressly advised him against it, leaving Frederick without the support he assumed would automatically be his. What he did require from James though was the £40,000 from Elizabeth's dowry to help fund his war effort, whether James liked it or not, he would be supporting his son-in-law.

On the other side of the argument was Federick's uncle, Maurice of Orange-Nassau. He had urged Frederick to take the crown from as early as September 1618, he even promised him all the financial backing he would need. But were his intentions coming from the right place? Maurice was looking to cause the new emperor trouble given that the 12-year truce between Spain and the Dutch Republic had come to an end. It would have been beneficial for him if Ferdinand was looking to deal with trouble in Bohemia rather than the Republic.

On 26 August 1619, Frederick was declared King of Bohemia, making Elizabeth his queen. When he heard the news that his ally Gabriel Bethlen, Prince of Transylvania, had taken Upper Austria (Modern day

Slovakia) his mind was made up. It was generally thought he was someone, as a Protestant, who could stand up against the might of the Catholic Habsburg empire. Upon acceptance of the crown the new king and queen, with their heir, Prince Frederick Henry, relocated to Prague. They sent Prince Charles Louis and Princess Elisabeth to live with relatives in Germany as a precaution along with their grandmother Louise Juliana.

As soon as they had arrived in Prague, Frederick left his wife and son to go and seal the oaths of allegiance and to rally his troops. Elizabeth was pregnant again and her isolation caused her mood to suffer and she plunged into long periods of depression; she had only just begun to feel at home in Heidelberg and now she had a whole new city to call home. Frederick misinterpreted Elizabeth's feelings as a lack of faith in him and his cause, so he wrote often reassuring her that he had not forgotten her and that she was the focus of his mind.

Frederick's rise to kingship meant he held two votes in the Electoral College and before long religious boundaries began to shift across the Holy Roman Empire. But as well as having influence over religion, being king now meant he could expand his borders and his finances. There was no doubt he was in a strong position; he knew Ferdinand could not raise an army to fight him and even without the support of England he still had the Protestant Union and United Provinces in his corner. As he went into his coronation, Frederick must have felt in a very strong position.

Frederick was crowned King of Bohemia on 4 November 1619 at St Vitus Cathedral, Prague with Elizabeth being crowned three days later with the crown of St Elizabeth of Hungary. As well as a crown and title, their accession also brought them war and it didn't take long for religion to become a sticking point. The Cathedral of St Vitus lies in the centre of Prague and had largely remained a place of catholic worship given the previous incumbents of the crown had been members of the Habsburg dynasty, but with the Calvinist Frederick now king, the catholic iconography was removed as per his orders. This was his first mistake, and sadly the first of many, as it showed a lack of tolerance. It could perhaps be argued the new king was just displaying his religious ideals but when he ordered the statues to be removed from the Charles

Bridge he was accused of a serious error of judgement. A monarch ought to promote religious tolerance like Ferdinand was offering under the Letters of Majesty but Frederick seems to have gone in hard and fast before thinking seriously about the consequences. But it wasn't just on grounds of religion where divides were becoming apparent. Elizabeth's English and Scottish ladies were also causing a stir after being accused of dressing inappropriately and for being too lively. Following the criticism, Elizabeth refused to alter hers or her ladies' ways which many of their new subjects thought was evil. Should Elizabeth have ceded some ground over this issue given their new status? Perhaps, but she had always been stubborn and believed that as her right as queen she alone would decide on how her household should behave.

Elizabeth's eldest son, the nearly 5-year-old, Prince Frederick Henry, had been the only child to accompany his parents to Prague, and he was elected as the successor to the crown by the General Assembly. It was important that the people could see their next king, having the heir with them proved to be a good piece of propaganda. On 17 December 1619, Elizabeth gave birth to her fourth child and third son who they named Prince Rupert. He was christened in Prague on 31 March 1620 at St Vitus Cathedral and the feasting afterwards along the riverside lasted an impressive seven hours. His godfather was Gabriel Bethlen, Prince of Transylvania, although his ambassador Imre Thurzo stood as proxy, the prince gifted Rupert a bejewelled black horse. On the face of it the birth of Rupert brought unity and stability but underneath, trouble was brewing.

Whilst the Bohemian princes backed and supported Frederick, the empire as a whole didn't and there were soon calls for his abdication. If he didn't comply with the emperor's wishes then he would be facing an imperial ban which would see him lose his Bohemian and German titles and lands leaving him and his family as outlaws. Frederick was a man of principle and his first duty was to protect his people, so, he chose to ignore the threats. The flip side of that was that it soon became inevitable war was on the horizon. Four Imperial armies were raised against Frederick, King James sent Sir Andrew Grey at the head of 2500 musketeers from Britain and a further 1200 soldiers would join them from the Bohemian border under the command of Lord Mansfeld. Ernst von Mansfeld had been born in Luxembourg which, at that time, formed part of the Spanish Netherlands and at the start of the Thirty Years' War he was one of the leading Generals on the battlefields and despite being a Roman Catholic he supported the Protestant cause. But don't be mistaken into thinking James was defending Frederick and his crown, he had not had a change of heart he still felt his son-in-law had made a mistake in taking the crown, for James this was about defending his daughter and grandchildren and probably more important, the royal house of Stuart, religion did not come into his decision to send help.

In January 1620, Elizabeth wrote to her father requesting more aid but he appeared to be stalling and it soon became clear to Elizabeth why. A potential marriage contract between Prince Charles and Ferdinand's niece, the Spanish Infanta Maria Anna, was being discussed and the king's advisors who supported the match did not want England to go into open war with Spain in case it damaged the prospect of a Spanish alliance. Instead, in a bid to avoid war and placate Elizabeth and Frederick, James sent Catholic and Protestant ministers to mediate between the two leagues to come to an agreement. Those talks resulted in the 1620 Treaty of Ulm. The treaty declared that no warfare was to take place within the Electoral lands of the empire, and the Protestant Union declared itself neutral. However, and rather bizarrely, the treaty did not include Frederick's Bohemian lands which left him open to attack and therefore rendered the treaty pointless. James was in a difficult position; he knew the only way to solve the issues engulfing the empire was war but he could not sanction any troops without calling Parliament and that was something he was loathe to do, in fact, throughout his 22-year reign James only called Parliament four times.

By mid-September, the situation had become desperate. Elizabeth was alone as her ladies-in-waiting had left Prague out of fear, but she was too proud to run and was adamant her place was beside Frederick on their thrones, despite his continuing pleas for her to leave. She did however see sense and send Prince Frederick Henry to safety. He was sent on a 44-day journey to Leeuwarden, the capital of Friesland. He was to reside with kinsman, Ernst Casimir of Nassau-Dietz, who would see to his education and keep him safe until the time came for him to return to court with his parents. He travelled in style at the head of a 4000-strong entourage and along the way he was treated to fine dining and lodgings. In some eyes, this was seen as a royal progress to allow Frederick Henry the opportunity to learn of the people of the Palatine and the lands that one day would be his, rather than a flight made in terror.

Back in Prague, Elizabeth had Prince Rupert to attend to, she continued to ignore pleas from Frederick to leave as she was determined to stay amongst the people she saw as her own, she felt an obligation to protect them but also it was perhaps better to keep your enemies in full view. Another reason she did not relish travel was because she was pregnant yet again and the prospect of a long journey must have felt daunting. She also argued she had no safe place to go and it was not certain she would even be given a safe passage to travel. She felt the prospect of being kidnapped by the emperor was too big of a risk, so in her mind, the best option was to stay put.

The biggest concern for Elizabeth was that her father had all but abandoned her and Frederick to their fate in Prague. But, back in England James declared that if the Spanish had not retreated by the Spring of 1621, he would wage war on Germany, the king had declared himself a supporter of the Palatinate but not Bohemia. This stance could not have been a surprise to Frederick; James had warned him against taking the Bohemian crown but he forged ahead regardless and now he was facing all-out war without the support of the English army and that was support he desperately needed.

On 8 November 1620, the Battle of White Mountain began. It was the decisive battle during the early stages of the Thirty Years' War and of Frederick's reign. Like any battle or war that was fought across Europe in the mid-fifteenth century, it was fundamentally down to religion. Catholics vs Protestants. The battle took place on the outskirts of Prague and saw the Bohemian forces led by Christian of Anhalt face up against those of the mighty Habsburgs under the command of Charles Bonaventure de Longueval. In terms of numbers, it was fairly even, the Protestant Union numbered approximately 21,000 men, whilst the emperor's men brought around 23,000 to the battle field. The battle was an unmitigated disaster for the Protestants and that largely came down to bad decision making by Anhalt. He boasted that the Habsburgs wouldn't come and fight in the cold winter weather but he misjudged them and they destroyed his troops by launching an aggressive attack. Despite the loss, the Bohemian forces did not suffer huge casualties, but they had no choice but to surrender. The defeat damaged their morale to the point that the opposition forces took Prague with little resistance. This defeat spelled the end for Frederick and Elizabeth as monarchs of Bohemia and they became known to history as the Winter King and Queen given the short time they had reigned. Not only was this a victory for Emperor Ferdinand, but it was a victory for the Catholics and provided the Counter Reformation the spring board it needed to launch itself across Europe. Elizabeth and Frederick may have been left wondering how much of a difference would help from James have made? We will never know of course, but knowing how well drilled the English forces were, they may have made a difference and the face of Europe may have taken on an entirely different look.

King Christian IV of Denmark was prevented from sending help to his stricken niece and her husband. He did not have an army ready to send into Bohemia and by the time he had mobilised his troops it was too late. It would also have meant he would be coming into direct confrontation with the Emperor Ferdinand and he was in no position to face that kind of challenge. With the war lost, Elizabeth and Frederick fled Prague but the enemy wasted no time and were hot on their tails and gaining ground fast. Elizabeth felt she was in so much danger that she decided to abandon the luggage train and mount a horse, which for a woman in her advanced stages of pregnancy was not recommended. In the November she wrote to her father telling him she would never abandon her husband and was willing to die beside him if she had to, what James thought of that we can only imagine. Maurice of Nassau wrote to Elizabeth to offer his commiserations on the loss of Prague but he also put a positive spin on things by celebrating their successful escape and declared he expected their triumphant return to the city with the year.

Frederick remained in Breslau, a city that had supported the Bohemian cause, whilst Elizabeth travelled on to safety in preparation for the birth of her fifth child. To reassure her, he made sure they remained in constant contact by letter but he seems to have forgotten his wife's situation as he was always encouraging her to keep moving and not to linger too long in one place. She spent two nights with Frederick's sister Elizabeth Charlotte but it was clear she was not welcome by the rest of the family, but sadly she had nowhere else to go. It was Elizabeth Charlotte's husband, the George William, the Elector of Brandenburg, who had previously written to Frederick requesting him not to send Elizabeth to them, his reasons were varied and included the fact they did not have enough supplies and the castle was a cold and draughty place. Naturally, he had other political reasons too, one being that the emperor had specifically requested he offer no help or refuge to his in-laws. George William tried to remain neutral but he was a weak man and his indecision put Elizabeth in a precarious position; she was near her time and needed somewhere to stay.

Frederick visited his wife in Küstrin but told her support for their cause was slowly dwindling. While he was there he spoke with James's advisor Edward Villers who pleaded with Frederick to give up his arms and the Bohemian crown, it appeared to pretty much everyone that he was fighting a losing battle and the in order to save face and remained dignified he ought to concede defeat. Three days after he left Elizabeth gave birth to a healthy son on 16 January 1621 whom they named Maurice. Elizabeth stayed with her newborn son for just over a month before leaving on 29 February. She left the baby in the care of his aunt and uncle and moved on to Wolfenbüttel where she was reunited with Frederick on 16 March. Together they travelled to the Dutch Republic, arriving at Arnhem on 28 March and from there they went to Rotterdam. Elizabeth then travelled to The Hague where a house, Kneuterdijk 22, had been made ready for the royal family to use. Having been without a home for five months, it would at last feel like somewhere to put down roots and reassess their situation. Fredrick had joined her there by April.

Many expected Elizabeth to return home to England whilst Frederick returned to the battlefield but James had ordered his daughter to remain on the continent, to return home would damage any help England could provide to Frederick. But it turned out The Hague was the perfect base for Frederick to launch further military attacks with the view of returning home to the Palatinate, for Elizabeth it provided a safe place for her children to finally be brought together.

Part IV

1621–1632

Still no help came from England. James wanted to help the Palatinate cause and even offered £500,000 of his own money to fund half the cost of a 30,000-strong army but Parliament were not willing to fund the rest. Sadly, the two sides could not reach a compromise. Elizabeth's frustrations were set to continue when she learnt James was in negotiations with her enemy Spain over a potential marriage between Prince Charles and the Infanta Maria. Regardless of when or where help was coming from the family had no choice but to settle in The Hague, a strategic city that sat at the heart of the States General of the Dutch Republic.

The house that was allocated to the family was considered to be on the small side but the location was convenient given that it was close to the Stadtholders residence. The large retinue that flocked to Elizabeth and Frederick had to find lodgings elsewhere. But as time went on it became clear that Elizabeth, Frederick and their children were there to stay and their court began to centre itself in The Hague. Furnishings were provided by many, including James. He sent chests, beds, gold and silver tapestries and velvet curtains from the Royal Wardrobe to help make their new exiled home more comfortable. To complete their home, they visited Amsterdam, where according to reports, they took a 'private' trip to visit the many merchants. It lasted eight days and had a train of over 100 people. They certainly were not hiding away in The Hague licking their wounds, and were determined to create a new court right at the heart of Holland.

The couple relied heavily on the States General for their upkeep and it didn't take long before their hosts began to resent the added expense they were burdened with by having the exiled royals at The Hague. Elizabeth and Frederick lived like the monarchs they no longer were and that lavish lifestyle cost a lot of money to maintain. In reality though they had very little choice, if they wanted to win back their lands and titles, to regain monarchical status, they had to rebuild their court and repair their reputation and all those things took time, money and good connections. But Elizabeth was impatient and began soliciting her father for military support but she was to be disappointed yet again as he declined to offer any kind of help. Instead, rather than the soldiers she desperately needed from him, he sent her a diamond-encrusted locket ring which held a miniature portrait of him. His treatment of Elizabeth began to draw criticism amongst his court as people began accusing him of abandoning his daughter and her family. The accusations hit James hard as he had always tried to be a good father, but like any king, the welfare of the nation came first and he felt he could spare no money or manpower to fight a cause that he had previously warned against. Unhappy with what he saw as unfair criticism, he had the dissenters arrested and imprisoned. Amongst the unhappy voices were the Earls of Southampton and Oxford but they very quickly released.

As life began to settle rivalries began to emerge, just as they had in Heidelberg. The Dutch countesses that had been recruited to attend Elizabeth were irked when Lucy, Countess of Bedford and Elizabeth's childhood friend, came to The Hague to visit. Lucy was the daughter of Elizabeth's beloved guardian Sir John Harington and was married to Edward Russell, Earl of Bedford. The earl had been embroiled in the ill-fated Essex Rebellion in 1601 against Elizabeth I and when the queen died Lucy acted quickly and rode hard to Scotland to present herself to Queen Anna. Amazingly, she managed to do this before any of the ladies appointed by the Privy Council arrived and gained herself a role in Queen Anna's household as Lady of the Bedchamber. She quickly became a loyal and trusted member of the court and travelled with the Queen, Prince Henry and Princess Elizabeth on their way to London. Lucy was immediately given precedence over all the other ladies putting Dutch noses out of joint. It is understandable why they felt aggrieved as they had worked hard to gain Elizabeth's trust and prove their loyalty to her only for that loyalty to be snubbed as soon as their English counterpart arrived. The bad feeling led to an unsettled court and when Lady Bedford's return voyage home was delayed due to bad weather, she refused to return to Elizabeth's residence. The atmosphere must have been volatile if she was willing to give up Elizabeth's company in the extra time she had been given.

In May 1621, the Protestant Union was formally dissolved on the orders of Emperor Ferdinand. Frederick's Imperial ban that had been imposed in the January also meant he had lost his right to elect a new emperor. Ferdinand replaced him with Maximilian I, Duke of Bavaria who he also appointed as the new Elector Palatine leading to Frederick losing his ancestral lands and titles. Frederick left The Hague in August 1621 to join the troops of Maurice, Prince of Orange, in Emmerich, Brandenburg. Elizabeth's cousin, Christian of Brunswick (their mothers were sisters), hoped to join the group and bring with him 1000 men to help bolster the numbers but it turned out he had an unhealthy obsession with her and claimed he was fighting for her sake only, he clearly felt a chivalric honour towards her. The Prince of Orange declined Brunswick's help on the advice of others but Frederick was desperate for men willing to fight for him and he was later admitted to the ranks. Victory came when a joint effort between Brunswick and the Count of Mansfeld, who Frederick had appointed to lead his army in Bohemia, joined together to bolster each other's forces. Frederick was able to briefly return to The Hague, albeit undercover, lest he be captured by the Spanish, so he donned a disguise and travelled as Sir Francis Nethersole's servant. Just days after he left the Republic in April 1622, Elizabeth gave birth to their second daughter, Louise Hollandine, a name which was granted by the States of Holland and one which gave the princess an annual gratuity of £200.

Despite the joy of the princess's birth news from the battlefield was not good. In June 1622, Brunswick waited patiently for Mansfeld to meet him with troops at Höchst, they were to combine their troops on the banks of the Main River at Darmstadt before moving on but the Catholic League was determined to block the meeting. By the 20 June, the Spanish troops arrived to find Brunswick's men already crossing the bridge at Höchst, he was vastly outnumbered and Tilly attempted to force Brunswick's men back over the bridge to isolate many of the protestant soldiers. But Brunswick ordered his men to withdraw over the bridge towards the town of Kelsterbach but the Catholics opened fire on them. It quickly became apparent to everyone theirs was a lost cause and panic set in. Brunswick's men stampeded the bridge over the River Main causing it to collapse after only 3000 men had managed to cross, the rest plunged into the icy water below, approximately 2000 men died. In total, Brunswick lost a third of his army whilst the baggage train and guns were looted by the Catholic troops. The Catholic army claimed victory based on the number of casualties (they lost about 100 men) but Brunswick had done what he set out to do and united his army with Mansfeld. The battle was a huge loss for Frederick and the Palatinate cause with the rest of his army openly failing to protect the borders. Frederick dismissed those left and they quickly joined the army of the Dutch Republic. On 19 September 1622, Heidelberg finally fell to the Emperor.

Frederick could not protect Elizabeth from the details of this devastating battle. He had successfully kept the nitty gritty details from her on previous occasions but this was different. As Elizabeth read the names of the deceased she saw those she recognised, those of husbands of her ladies-in-waiting. It brought the war and death right to her doorstep. Elizabeth Dudley had only been married to her husband Johann Kasimir, Count Löwenstein-Scharffeneck for a matter of months before he perished in the River Main. She never took another husband, instead, she devoted her life to serving Elizabeth and stayed with her for a further forty years. Following the disaster Mansfeld was discharged from his post and persistent rumours of disloyalty clung to him. Frederick had no choice but to return to The Hague where six months after her birth he met his daughter Louise Hollandine.

With everything but Frankenthal lost Elizabeth felt abandoned and betrayed by her father putting the English ambassadors in a precarious position. Whilst there were some English forces fighting for the Palatinate cause under the leadership of Horace Vere, 1st Baron Vere of Tilbury, the numbers weren't what Elizabeth or Frederick thought was enough. Vere had been sent by James to the Palatinate in 1620 and conducted himself with courage and bravery which did not go unnoticed back home in England. Many felt empathy for Elizabeth and the dire circumstances she and her family now found themselves in but they also had a duty to King and country and that duty came with a sting in the tail. James commanded that Frankenthal, the town that formed part of Elizabeth's marriage settlement, was to be handed over to the Spanish, a gift from James directly to his daughter's enemy. Sir John Burroughs, an English officer under the command of Vere, had strived the best he could to keep hold of Frankenthal for Elizabeth but when the order came from home he had little choice but to surrender it to Spanish commander, Francisco Verdugo, which he reluctantly did on 14 April 1623. No doubt the surrender of her beloved Frankenthal left a bitter taste in the mouths of Elizabeth and her supporters.

Frederick had agreed to a truce with Ferdinand which brought to an end the 'Palatine Phase' of the Thirty Years' War. But Brunswick continued to fight for the Bohemian and Palatinate cause as his loyalty knew no bounds. He declined Ferdinand's offer of a truce in exchange for a full pardon; he was no longer part of Frederick's army and was free to fight for whoever and wherever he liked. This meant he could continue to fight on their behalf and there was no risk of breaking of any truce that had been already agreed. Brunswick, and Mansfeld for that matter, were not bound by any pre-existing truce.

It was to turn out that actions back home in England were to play an active part in Elizabeth's situation. Her younger brother Prince Charles and the Duke of Buckingham had left London for Madrid intending to bring his Spanish bride, Infanta Maria, back to London. In order to travel unimpeded, they had to do so incognito so they donned disguises and false names, deciding to travel as the Smith brothers wearing false beards. This was a foolish thing to do, if Charles's true identity had become known he risked kidnap or even worse, murder. Any one of England's enemies could have intercepted the pair and held them for ransom and thereby putting James in a very tricky situation. But it was the only action Charles could think of to help his sister as he felt the diplomatic route would be more advantageous than warfare, which had so far failed in restoring Elizabeth and Frederick to their rightful places. The deal was that part of the Spanish match between England and Spain was the restoration of the Palatinate, Spain got a covetous match with England and Elizabeth and Frederick got their lands and titles restored to them.

The risks taken by Charles were undoubtedly chivalric but if he had been discovered and murdered it would have brought Elizabeth one step closer to the throne of England which was something the Holy Roman Empire could not ignore. The combined force of England, Bohemia and the Palatinate would place the Emperor in a very vulnerable position and Charles's trip frightened the Spanish for that very reason and so when he arrived in Spain and his true identity revealed the Spanish knew they had to keep him safe. James on the other hand hoped these fears would bring a swift and positive conclusion to the match and preferably before the hot Spanish summer began. The Spanish however felt the restoration of the Palatinate would take much longer to negotiate given the complex nature of the lands and estates under discussion. The match with Catholic Spain was deeply unpopular in England to the point that Elizabeth was being considered as a potential replacement for James leading to rumours quickly spreading that she was about to arrive in England which would force her father back to Scotland leaving her the undisputed ruler of England. Elizabeth refused to acknowledge these rumours as she probably knew the chances of her sitting on England's throne were pretty slim and the talk was nothing but speculation. Prince Charles left Spain without his bride and as a show of affection and solidarity to his older sister he cut off a lock of his hair and sent it to her, which she would wear in an earring from her left ear. The failure of the Spanish match was a cause of relief and happiness for Elizabeth and Frederick and celebrations were enjoyed across The Hague.

Elizabeth and Frederick knew the chances of reclaiming their lands were all but gone so they decided to put down firmer roots in the Dutch Republic. The older children had been scattered across Europe for their own protection since they left Heidelburg. Charles Louis and Elisabeth had made their way to Berlin in the custody of their aunt Catherine and grandmother Louise Juliana whilst Maurice, the baby born in Küstrin, remained in the care of his aunt and uncle, the Electress and Elector of Brandenburg. Frederick Henry and Rupert had been with their parents along with their baby sister Louise Hollandine since their arrival at The Hague. Elizabeth was pregnant for the seventh time and it was decided the children should be brought together to live under one roof and hold their own court. Permission was sought from the Mayor of Leiden and the Prince of Orange to set up the household after they found the ideal residence, a house in Leiden which belonged to the Prince of Orange.

The three children who already lived at The Hague with their parents would move there first under the governance of Monsieur de Plessen and his wife. The grand building was called the Prinsenhof and lay just three hours from The Hague. In June 1623, the children moved in with Charles Louis joining them by March 1624. In August of 1624, Elizabeth gave birth to another son they called Louis, sadly he was only to live for four months, he died on Christmas Eve later that year. In September, Frederick Henry enrolled at Leiden University as life at the Prinsenhof settled into routine. The very idea of the children's court was more than likely Elizabeth's idea given her close relationship with her elder brother Henry Frederick. They were often forced to separate which caused great upset to both children so Elizabeth wanted to ensure that by having all her children in one residence meant none of them would be alone at any one time as they would always have constant companions and be surrounded by the love of their siblings. Some may see this as a risky thing to do, should disaster befall the residents it could see the destruction of their heirs.

The education of her children was also something Elizabeth took very seriously and as the children of exiled parents it would be more than likely they would need to enter service of some sort. The boys would be more than likely to take a career in the armed forces and maybe the younger sons would enter the church and that kind of education would be left to those with experiences but she personally oversaw the education of her daughters. Teaching them multiple languages was important, but crucially she made sure they were taught the same subjects as their brothers other than the physical martial subjects. Many other tutors were brought in including John Dinley who became tutor to Frederick Henry, James gave his permission for Dinley to leave England to take up the post as long as he ensured his grandchildren were taught all about England and their place within it, it was paramount they were educated in their British heritage.

Life at the Prinsenhof was regimented. The children would rise at 7 am for prayers and reading and had to be dressed by 8:30 am when they would attend their lessons until 10 am. From 10–11 am they would attend dancing classes following which they would have their midday meal which would require strict etiquette. Following lunch, the girls would rest, and learn to sew or embroider whilst the boys learnt all about warfare. Lessons would resume at 2 pm and would last until 6 pm when they would take supper. At 8.30 pm the children would go to bed with Bible reading and prayers before they retired for the night. If their parents were in residence they would seek their blessings before bed, if not, their governess or nursemaids would make sure everyone was safe in bed by the required time.

By the end of 1623, talk of marriage for Frederick Henry began to circulate. Maximilian I, Duke of Bavaria and new ruler of the upper Palatinate suggested his niece as a possible bride. A match with Frederick Henry would have created an eighth electorate and made them a greater force against the Holy Roman Empire. The proposal was sent to London rather than The Hague but the issue was in London no one could actually verify if the duke even had a niece that was his to marry off. News of the proposal and the way it was announced worried Elizabeth and Frederick, but James assured his daughter the match would never be sanctioned because his grandson was a far too valuable commodity for the king to marry off so lightly. Until Prince Charles married and had a legitimate heir of his own it was highly likely Frederick Henry could be King of England, Ireland and Scotland.

The Spanish match was dead in the water and Europe stood on the brink of war. In England, accusations from the Spanish ambassador, Juan de Mendoza, Marquis of Inojosa, circulated that Charles, Buckingham and other members of the council were plotting to remove James unless he agreed to go to war with Spain. Letters were sent to James which named Buckingham as the chief conspirator but more worryingly was the accusation that Elizabeth and her secretary, Sir Francis Nethersole, had gone about purposefully wrecking the Spanish match and were working to have Frederick Henry marry Buckingham's daughter Mary. The plot aimed to direct the line of succession of the British thrones down through Elizabeth's line rather than Charles's and the end of the Spanish interest was a benefit to Elizabeth. As for Buckingham, it meant his daughter would one day be Queen Consort but his grandchild would become the monarch.

Any attempt to alter the line of succession amounted to treason. Naturally, Elizabeth declared herself innocent of any wrongdoing but someone designed the plot to make it look like Elizabeth was the chief conspirator and on the face of it looked like she was offering her son to Buckingham's daughter in exchange for him sabotaging the Spanish negotiations in Madrid. Nethersole had been in Spain at the same time as Charles and Buckingham and was even given letters to carry on to Elizabeth in The Hague, had someone seen an opportunity to create mischief? It does seem like a coincidence that the rumours started with the Spanish Ambassador. Whether the match between Frederick Henry and Mary Villiers was genuine is unknown, but we do know portraits were exchanged which was seen as an important step in the process of marriage negotiations in royal circles. It also remained a persistent rumour that dogged Elizabeth and no matter how hard she tried to convince her father she was innocent of any wrongdoing it kept rearing its ugly head. Eventually the accusations made by Inojosa were dismissed and brought shame and disgrace to the Spanish as meddling with another country's line of succession was considered and ill-judged move.

On 6 October 1624, following a four-hour labour Elizabeth gave birth to her eighth child, a son named Edward. The happiness brought by the birth of the new baby was soon dampened when one of Elizabeth and Frederick's closest allies, Maurice, Prince of Orange, lay dying in The Hague. Maurice had been a pivotal part of Frederick's life and played an influential role in his acceptance of the Bohemian crown. Further bad news came when Henry Wriothesley, Earl of Southampton and champion of Elizabeth succumbed to a fever on 10 November 1624 at Bergen-op-Zoom at the age of 51. Tragically, just five days before, his son James had died of an unspecified fever at Roosendaal. They were buried together on 28 December 1624 at their home Titchfield Abbey.

To compound their grief even further Elizabeth and Frederick lost their son Louis who had been suffering from illness for about a month that had been brought on by teething, he was just 4 months old. Despite the high infant mortality rates of the time, he was the first of their children to die. There must have been significant concerns for his health as he was brought to The Hague to be closer to his parents who were at his side when he breathed his last. Letters were written to James to request details of the burial as Elizabeth and Frederick felt the churches in The Hague were unsuitable due to the vast numbers of bodies that already lay in the vaults. Elizabeth wanted her baby to be buried in England alongside his grandmother Queen Anna but James refused this request and so the young prince was laid to rest at the Church of Delft not far from the remains of his paternal great grandfather William the Silent, Prince of Orange.

Not long after burying her baby son, Elizabeth was confronted with the news that her father had passed away. King James VI/I died on 27 March 1625 at Theobalds House, Hertfordshire. He had been suffering from arthritis before finally succumbing to a stroke. James and Elizabeth had a somewhat complex relationship which altered dramatically after she married. It is without question that he cared for his daughter but he was a king, and a pragmatic one at that. He saw Elizabeth as a very useful political tool that he was able to use to position himself at the heart of Europe. But when it came to the crunch, the good of the nation came before the welfare of his daughter. James was never keen on war and put his desire for peace above her feelings. Elizabeth always felt her father should have supported her and Frederick more than he did which led to feelings of disappointment on her part. Regardless of the supposed lack of support she remained loyal to her father and he took great pleasure in his grandchildren and the continued legacy of the Royal House of Stuart that Elizabeth spread throughout the courts of Europe.

The news that her father had died and her brother was now king reached Elizabeth on 6 April which gave her renewed sense of optimism that he would be more supportive than their father had been. Despite losing her father it was the death of her 'second father' Maurice, Prince of Orange on the 23 April that had a more profound impact on Elizabeth with his death she had lost a supportive and loving confidante. He was laid to rest beside baby Louis at the Church of Delft. In Maurice's place came his half-brother Frederick Henry. At the time he became Prince of Orange, Frederick Henry married Elizabeth's Lady, Amalia of Solms-Braunfels in the hope he might have an heir at the request of Maurice. She also became his leading political advisor and took on the supporting role of regent when her husband became too ill to perform his duties.

Back in England, it had become clear the new king, Charles I, would not marry into Spain, instead, he took Henrietta Maria as his bride when they married in May 1625. She was the youngest daughter of King Henry IV of France and his Italian wife Marie de Medici which meant she was a catholic, making her unpopular with the English. It also meant she could not be crowned in a Church of England service so she never had a coronation. Charles's marriage, whilst not a Spanish one, still irked Elizabeth as it meant she and her children would be displaced in the line of succession by their children. Still, she was hopeful her younger brother would aid her far more than her father ever did and so she made all the right noises when it came to his choice of bride. The early indications were that it was the king's aim to restore his sister and brother-in-law to the crown of Bohemia and reinstate them in the Palatinate which no doubt brought great cheer to them in The Hague. But to Elizabeth and Frederick, the Palatinate was more important as the Electorate had a certain worth attached to it but they still refused to give up their Bohemian titles for if they did it would indicate Frederick's election was flawed and invalid and the Imperial ban which stripped him of his lands was fair and just.

Along with the news of their father's death, Charles also gave orders that the English and Mansfeld were to obey Frederick in all things. Charles was to help relieve the situation in Breda with the aid of the Dutch States;

the king of England was certainly making all the right noises which filled Elizabeth with renewed hope. By May 1625, Stadtholder Frederick Henry made attempts to send fresh provisions to Breda, he did so by attacking one of the Empire's army bases, sadly they faced defeat and the defiant Breda fell to the empire on 5 June 1625. The siege lasted eight months and saw 13,000 men die. With the loss of life so great the number of men able to lead the command decreased, out of the ten English officers only two were left. The Dutch had suffered greatly too and Mansfeld saw huge losses too but his men remained stoic and saw the decimation of his army as nothing but an inconvenience, not to mention the £250,000 his failed expedition cost. At this point, Elizabeth and Frederick were as far away as ever from regaining their Palatinate lands.

In the spring of 1625, news reached The Hague that King Charles was preparing a fleet to attack Spain by intercepting their ships which were sailing back from the Americas all of which were laden with gold and treasure. It was hoped that an assault on the trade routes and the taking of the loot would cause Spain a significant monetary loss that would then force them to relinquish the Palatinate. Elizabeth and Frederick appointed Buckingham to be their Admiral of the sea meaning he could lead the expedition, that turned out to be a grave mistake on their part. Buckingham's popularity had been on a steady decline and was continuing on a downward trajectory so he promptly handed over the responsibility of the expedition to Sir Edward Cecil, Viscount Wimbledon and Robert Devereaux, the 3rd Earl of Essex who became vice-admiral. Whilst these two men had shown their loyalty to Elizabeth and had seen success on the battlefield neither had any experience in leading an attack at sea and that inexperience was going to prove their downfall.

By September 1625, Charles and the States General had agreed on their offensive. A total of 84 ships had been prepared and manned with English men ready to fight for Elizabeth and Frederick, unfortunately, the men and a vast number of the ships were ill-equipped. Regardless of the state of the fleet the English, along with 20 Dutch ships, set sail from Plymouth Harbour in October 1625 heading south for the Spanish port of Cadiz. Cecil's expedition was an abject failure with men that were ill-disciplined and delinquent but the book stopped with Buckingham in his capacity of Lord High Admiral. The ships limped home to Plymouth with approximately 2000 men less than they had set sail with. Those missing had been killed by the Spanish whilst they were drunk in Fort Puntales while on the hunt for wine and women. But things were no better for those who had managed to get back on board and sail for home for when they arrived back they found Plymouth held little reserves for them and many died on home soil of starvation and disease. A very sad state of affairs for the country with reported to have the finest navy in the world.

Buckingham returned to The Hague to build a wider alliance beyond the English and Dutch. He wanted to include the German states, Denmark and Sweden and he was successful in creating a new coalition that became known as The Treaty of the Hague. The treaty was signed on 9 December 1625 between England, the Dutch Estates and Denmark and under the new treaty it was agreed that England and the Dutch would provide funds to Christian IV of Denmark help support his campaigns during the Thirty Years' War. Charles showed his support by providing the funds needed to raise enough troops to regain the Palatinate but Buckingham felt they needed more and so visited Amsterdam to pawn some items from the crown jewels. He failed to achieve the necessary amounts and the jewels were returned to the English court. As the treaty was being negotiated, the terms agreed upon and the funds raised, Elizabeth and Frederick sat and patiently waited in The Hague.

On 7 July 1626, Elizabeth gave birth to a daughter they called Henriette, named after Queen Henrietta Maria. Back home in England, trouble was brewing for Buckingham as he was accused by parliament as the man behind the Cadiz disaster. He faced charges of corruption and worse still, high treason. Charles dissolved parliament before any further action could be taken against his favourite and that unfortunately meant no further money for the Palatinate cause. Seeing as he had already pawned smaller items from the crown jewels he decided to raid his nobles, if they didn't or were not willing to pay up he threatened them with imprisonment. The king seemed to be taking his sister's plight seriously and left no avenue unexplored when it came to raising the funds to face down Ferdinand II and the Holy Roman Empire.

The Palatinate cause suffered a major blow when Elizabeth's cousin and most loyal leader the Christian, Duke of Brunswick died at the age of 26. Ever the chivalric soldier ready to fight for honour and a sense of adventure he died of fever probably brought on by an untreated wound and poor conditions that came with life as a soldier.

But out of the gloom came a rare glimpse of hope in the form of Bethlen Gabor, Prince of Transylvania and with him came troops of men willing to fight for Elizabeth and Frederick. A fierce enemy of Ferdinand II he was keen to enter the fray in an attempt to regain his lands in upper Hungary. At last, it looked like the Palatinate cause had been bolstered, Gabor despised the emperor and the empire and he would have been happy to see them fall but sadly this road to victory failed when Gabor made peace with the emperor in December 1626 dealing Elizabeth and Frederick another blow. News came through that Mansfeld had died meaning the cause had lost yet another able and loyal leader. He had been ill for some time but that didn't stop him from taking to the battlefield one last time. From Hungary, he set out for Venice but once he had reached Sarajevo his health took a turn for the worse. He knew he was dying and as a lifelong soldier he donned his armour and delivered one final speech to the troops that stayed had with him. It is said he died standing up in his armour at sunrise on 14 December 1626, he was buried in Split, in modern day Croatia.

Determined to get things moving again, Buckingham led further campaigns in the Stuart-Franco wars but sadly they all proved to be disastrous and his continuing failures turned the public against him. The king had managed to save him from charges of treason but he was public enemy number one and Charles could not protect his friend from the wrath of his own men. The ever-unpopular George Villiers, Duke of Buckingham met his end on 23 August when he was fatally stabbed. John Felton was an army officer who felt Buckingham had overlooked him for promotion due to injuries he had sustained in earlier campaigns. With a serious grudge he took his opportunity to end his enemy whilst the two men were at The Greyhound pub in Plymouth. Felton had been praised for his actions whilst Buckingham had been described as effeminate and corrupt. Felton was hailed as a courageous and fearless soldier. He may have been lauded as a hero amongst the people but the king wanted revenge and Felton was later executed for his crime. He was hung on 29 November 1628 and his body was taken to Portsmouth and put on display for all to see. Buckingham was buried in Westminster Abbey where he rests in a lavish tomb, he was 35 years old and left a wife and three children. As the king's favourite he was not widely mourned, Elizabeth mourned for the sake of her brother but deep down she was unmoved by his death.

The cause quietened and so did life at The Hague. Elizabeth and Charles exchanged portraits of one another as tokens of sibling love and affection. Elizabeth's also served as a constant visual reminder to Charles that his sister was in need of support and most importantly, cash. Their dire financial circumstances meant Elizabeth and Frederick could no longer fully support their households in the way they wished to and cuts would have to be made. The year ended on a positive note when Elizabeth gave birth on 19 December, it was the couple's eleventh child, a daughter they named Charlotte. Further good news came the new Admiral and Captain-General of the Dutch West India Company, Piet Pieterzoon Hein, finally captured a Spanish fleet in the Caribbean. He triumphantly sailed the captured galleons back to Holland with booty including gold, silver and other expensive trading goods. He stopped at The Hague on his journey to Amsterdam and whilst there, he dined with Frederick and the Prince of Orange and invited both men to come and view the treasure in Amsterdam. There was more to this than just glory for Frederick though as he had inherited an eighth of the loot from shares passed on by Maurice.

At Elizabeth's encouragement Frederick decided to take Frederick Henry with him, in the hope that fresh air and adventure would be good for the young man who up until recently had been feeling unwell, he had returned to The Hague from Leiden as he wanted the attention of his mother. Frederick was persuaded and the pair left The Hague at 6 am on 17 January and from there they travelled to Haarlem where they hired a barge that would sail them to Amsterdam via the IJ, a notoriously difficult waterway given the sand banks at either side. At Zaandam, their barge was hit by another vessel and immediately capsized. Frederick was pulled to safety along with six other men but sadly ten drowned including Prince Frederick Henry. His body was found the following morning still clinging to the mast of the ship. On 19 January Frederick brought the body of his son home to The Hague where he lay in state, his face was bruised from the mast but the rest of his body remained unmarked. He was then embalmed and interred in the Kloosterkerk in The Hague, the death of their eldest child and heir devastated Elizabeth and Frederick, she refused to write any letters during her period of intense grief and Frederick's health was never the same again from the guilt he felt that he could not save his son, and that he had survived.

The death of Frederick Henry now meant Charles Louis was the heir to the Palatinate Electorship, but if and when he would ever inherit the estates was uncertain, but thanks to the taking of the Spanish ships the Dutch now had the funds to take on the might of the Emperor's army. As Elizabeth tried to come to terms with her grief news reached her that Henrietta Maria was pregnant and whilst the news was welcome in England it was met with a frosty reception in The Hague. The unborn child represented a threat to Elizabeth and her children; it marked a potential loss of power and importance. Charles may be less inclined to fight for the Palatinate cause if their position in the line of succession for England was less important. Sadly, the pregnancy ended in a miscarriage but Henrietta Maria would eventually go on to provide England with its heir and a spare. Charles became more inclined to build better relations with his wife's home nation France and so he brought the Franco-Stuart conflict to an end in 1629. Elizabeth had already lost many of her loyal leaders and Generals and now her brother looked to be shifting away from the Palatinate cause as well. Charles was also brokering for peace between Spain and the Dutch which he felt would help bring about the restoration of Frederick and later Charles Louis. But suddenly out of nowhere, the powerful Swedes became involved in the conflict with King

1. Princess Elizabeth Stuart, aged six, by Robert Peake. (*via Wikimedia Commons*)

2. Princess Elizabeth Stuart, aged ten, by Robert Peake the Elder. (*via Wikimedia Commons*)

3. James VI of Scotland and I of England by John de Critz. (*via Wikimedia Commons*)

4. Anna of Denmark by John de Critz. (*via Wikimedia Commons*)

6. Mary, Queen of Scots. (*via Wikimedia Commons*)

5. Henry Stuart, Lord Darnley, and his brother, Lord Charles Stuart by Hans Eworth. (*via Wikimedia Commons*)

7. Prince Henry Frederick, Prince of Wales by Robert Peake. (*via Wikimedia Commons*)

8. Frederick, Elector Palatine, in 1613, by Michiel Jansz van Mierevelt. (*via Wikimedia Commons*)

9. Portrait of Elizabeth Stuart, Queen of Bohemia by Michiel Jansz van Mierevelt. (*via Wikimedia Commons*)

10. Prince Frederick Henry, Crown Prince of the Palatinate, by Jan Anthonisz van Ravesteyn. (*via Wikimedia Commons*)

11. Prince Charles Louis, Elector Palatine by Anthony van Dyck. (*via Wikimedia Commons*)

12. Elisabeth of the Palatinate by Gerard van Honthorst. (*via Wikimedia Commons*)

13. Prince Rupert of the Rhine (right) and Charles Louis, Elector Palatine (left), in 1637, by Anthony van Dyck. (*via Wikimedia Commons*)

14. Prince Rupert, Duke of Cumberland by Peter Lely. (*via Wikimedia Commons*)

15. Prince Maurice of the Palatinate, Artist Unknown.
(*via Wikimedia Commons*)

16. Louise Hollandine, Self Portrait.
(*via Wikimedia Commons*)

17. Edward of the Palatinate in Armour by Gerard van Honthorst. (*via Wikimedia Commons*)

18. Henriette Marie of the Palatinate by Gerard van Honthorst. (*via Wikimedia Commons*)

19. Philip Frederick of the Palatinate by Cornelis Janssens van Ceulen. (*via Wikimedia Commons*)

20. Princess Sophia of the Palatinate, by Gerard van Honthorst. (*via Wikimedia Commons*)

21. Elisabeth and Gustavus Adolphus of the Palatinate by Gerard van Honthorst, in 1636. (*via Wikimedia Commons*)

22. Frederick V, Elector of the Palatinate and King of Bohemia by Michiel Jansz van Mierevelt. (*via Wikimedia Commons*)

23. Portrait of Elizabeth Stuart, Queen of Bohemia by Gerard von Honthorst. (*via Wikimedia Commons*)

24. Elizabeth Stuart, Queen of Bohemia, as a widow by Gerard van Honthorst, in 1642. (*via Wikimedia Commons*)

25. Sophia, Electress of Hanover, by Gerard van Honthorst. (*via Wikimedia Commons*)

26. Triumph of the Winter Queen Allegory of the Just, 1636, Gerard van Honthorst. (*via Wikimedia Commons*)

27. St Vitus Cathedral, Prague. (© *Chris Adams*)

28. St Vitus Cathedral, Prague. (© *Chris Adams*)

29. Sophia Dorothea and her two children, George (Future George II of Great Britain) and Sophia Dorothea (Future Queen of Prussia) by Jaques Vaillant. (*via Wikimedia Commons*)

30. Sophia, Dowager Electress of Hanover, Artist Unknown. (*via Wikimedia Commons*)

31. King George I of Great Britain by Wilhelm Fontaine, 1720s. (*via Wikimedia Commons*)

Gustavus Adolphus's army arriving at Usedom in July 1630. He then became a rallying point for all the Protestant princes and led a successful campaign against the Catholic empire at the Battle of Breitenfeld in 1631.

As war raged, Elizabeth gave birth to her daughter Sophia on 14 October 1630 but her birth was tinged with sadness as baby Charlotte died on 14 January 1631 at the age of just 2 years old following a long illness. In the November of 1631, the Swedes decided to take a more decisive role in the war on the side of the Protestants and as an offer of thanks Elizabeth and Frederick named their thirteenth and final child Gustavus Adolphus after Sweden's great king. King Gustavus Adolphus personally intervened in the Thirty Years' War in June 1630 at which point he had just over 4000 troops under his command. But thanks in part to French money and back up soldiers from Sweden he led a successful assault through Northern Germany. In September 1631, he won a decisive battle against Tilly at the Battle of Breitenfeld after which he headed for the banks of the Rhine where he set up his headquarters for the winter months. When the fighting season began in March 1632, and with a disgruntled Frederick in the ranks, an assault was made on the great Habsburg ally Bavaria he then put down the Catholic stronghold following the Battle of Rain. King Gustavus Adolphus was a fearless warrior king who entered battle without any armour for he believed God would be all the protection he needed.

King Gustavus Adolphus died on 6 November 1632 during the Battle of Lutzen. He received a bullet to his left arm and his horse one to its neck. In his confusion he became separated from his troops and somehow managed to end up behind enemy lines where he was shot in the back and stabbed causing him to fall from his horse. As he lay on the ground he received one final gunshot to the head. His men found his partially naked body over two hours later. They removed him from the battlefield on the back of a Swedish gun carriage.

Frederick had joined King Gustavus Adolphus's army in February 1632 but the good feeling did not last long when the Swedes declared Frederick was not to lead an army of his own, leading to a breakdown of the once good-natured alliance. This marked the start of twelve months of bickering over the Palatinate, the English were keen to forge an English-Swedish alliance in an attempt to finally solve the issue. Everyone was on the same side yet to Frederick he felt more isolated than ever before.

For Elizabeth, the ultimate loss came at 7 am on 29 November 1632 when Frederick died. His health had never really recovered following the death of Frederick Henry and he was struck down by fever whilst in Mainz. Following a state of delirium he fell unconscious before passing away. The news was purposely kept from Elizabeth for ten days as her own health had been troubled, she felt she was suffering from a similar fever to Frederick and it was thought the news about her husband could be potentially dangerous to her health. Elizabeth and Frederick's marriage had been a long and happy union which saw the birth of thirteen children. She had been a loving and supportive wife who had encouraged her husband in all his endeavours, including the taking of the Bohemian crown she also remained loyal to him when he subsequently lost the throne just a year later. Elizabeth Stuart was everything a royal wife ought to have been, she was obedient and dedicated but above all else she provided him with multiple heirs. All this was not to say that she was meek and mild, when it came to her marriage, as with the arguments over precedence, she was not afraid to speak her mind if she felt an injustice had taken place, a trait her father had admired in her.

King Charles's first point of action was to request Elizabeth and her children return home to England to live at his court as part of the Stuart royal family. Elizabeth had other plans; she needed to remain in The Hague to fight for her children's inheritance. Frederick's death meant the 14-year-old Charles Louis now took up the fight for the Palatinate lands.

Part V

1632–1649

Following Frederick's death Elizabeth seemed to reinvent herself as a determined mother hell-bent on protecting and advancing her many children. She had a complex relationship with her children but she was an ambitious mother and raised them under difficult circumstances given the majority had been born and raised in exile. Regardless of her financial constraints she strived to give them the best opportunities she could and even though she was grieving the loss of Frederick she realised that in order to advance her children she had to remain at the forefront of European politics. However, she was in a precarious position as she had lost her father, husband and many of her loyal leaders and with a brother in England she was open to manipulation from those wanting to interfere in the regency of Charles Louis. Her priority following Frederick's death was to ensure Charles Louis had an Electorship to govern when he reached his majority, the determination to regain the Palatinate lands did not diminish with Frederick's death, if anything she became more determined to correct the wrongs that had been done to the family. Elizabeth had been fighting for years to help her husband win back his birthright and she understood the fight was still far from won, there was no way she would walk away now, she was committed to the fight and therefore declined Charles's offer to return to England. But away from politics and talk of war was a woman in mourning and even eighteen months after Frederick's death her home was still draped in black, she even had stationery edged with black although as with other traumatic events in her life her ferocious letter writing did decrease in volume.

Elizabeth's decision to remain in The Hague meant she not only had physical distance from Charles but also political distance, how Charles felt about his sister's refusal to return home is unclear but he would have rued the opportunity to have her closer to him and under his control. She was now free to make her own choices concerning the running of her households and the future of the Palatinate. The relationship between Elizabeth and Charles was never as close as it was with Henry Frederick before his death but it began to suffer even further as Charles began to mistrust his elder sister and things were about to get worse.

The Swedes demanded payment for their newly conquered Frankenthal and Charles gave his permission for voluntary donations to be taken. The deal that had been struck was that the Swedes would hand over Frankenthal to Charles Louis's Palatinate administrator the Duke of Simmern. To clinch the deal, Nethersole had looked to borrow against the money that had already been pledged but Charles wanted the deal kept quiet so if the news leaked that Nethersole was making deals to help secure the Palatinate it risked him being exposed and would put him under increasing pressure to declare war against Spain. Unfortunately, that is what happened as word got out that Nethersole had secured the monies before any legal documentation had been drawn up; worse still, to cover his tracks, he accused a member of Queen Henrietta Maria's household of being the source of the leak but this only angered the queen and she took him to court for accusing her servant which by default meant he was accusing her of wrongdoing too. The outcome was not favourable for Nethersole and Elizabeth was advised to dismiss him, whilst she was incensed at the treatment of her secretary she was powerless to help him. The whole plan to buy back part of the Palatinate imploded and Elizabeth was back to square one not only had another opportunity gone begging but she had lost her loyal secretary and angered her brother in the process. Nethersole's punishment was a stay in the Tower of London, permanent exile from Elizabeth's court and banishment from the Stuart court in London. He was eventually released and spent much of his time on his lands in Polesworth, Warwickshire from there he was vocal in his support of the king during the Civil War and spent much of his time writing pamphlets urging for a peaceful solution to be found. Charles was sending a clear message to his court, if anyone openly criticised him or showed loyalty to Elizabeth over him then they would not be welcome at his court. He seemed determined to incapacitate his sister and her household and because of his actions, Frankenthal and Heidelberg remained under Swedish command. Thankfully by October they had become bored and gone home providing the French with an opportunity to seize Heidelberg and they were in league with Bavaria, Elizabeth's arch enemy. This now meant the Upper Palatinate and the titles that went with it were in Bavarian hands with French protection meaning once more she was thwarted.

Charles Louis turned 18 years old in 1635 which meant he could legally assume the governorship of the Palatinate but as he was exiled from his homeland he offered his services to his uncle, King Charles instead. He arrived at Gravesend in November along with a retinue of about seventy men. The sending of Charles Louis to England was a calculated move on Elizabeth's part as talk of a possible investiture of the Electorship at the Stuart court circulated and she hoped it would shake the council and Bishops into action and by that she hoped they would agree to provide the Elector with an army to help him fight for his rights. But like so many times before, Elizabeth misjudged the situation and no investiture was undertaken.

In February 1636 Charles Louis was joined by his younger brother Prince Rupert and both young men were warmly welcomed at their uncle's court and many lavish entertainments were put on for their enjoyment. They were at an age where they needed to hone and perfect their military abilities and Elizabeth gave express orders that if the British army was to refuse them training they were to return home immediately and take up their training with the Prince of Orange's men. The issue was England was not willing to let the two brothers leave the country knowing they were going home to take up arms against Spain.

The fight for the Palatinate and Charles Louis's birth right continues to rage on as Elizabeth met with Thomas Howard, 14th Earl of Arundel who passed through The Hague on his way to peace talks in Vienna. Howard had been sent by Charles to negotiate for peace on behalf of Charles Louis. He instructed him to seek a lift of the Imperial ban that had been placed on Frederick in 1621 if he could not secure a full restoration for his nephew. This displeased Elizabeth as she wanted a full restoration to all the lands and titles that were rightfully her sons and she was not willing to accept anything less than that, it looked like brother and sister disagreed yet again but Elizabeth seems to have not fully understood that a full, or even partial, restoration was not going to happen based on that one request alone, she does come across as somewhat naïve to think that after fifteen years Ferdinand II was not going to gift the lands back. That said, things started to look promising again when Wilhelm V, Landgrave of Hesse and Bernard, Duke of Saxe-Weimer joined Charles Louis in his fight and they urged the king to allow the two Palatine brothers to recruit soldiers from across his realm. Charles refused this request along with a request for financial aid as he did not agree with his sister that Charles Louis could continue to take the war to Germany, was Charles of the thinking that they should let the lands and title go? The king's stance was clear in that he didn't want to engage in open warfare with Spain or at least he didn't want to until the Stuart-Franco alliance had been agreed. Naturally Elizabeth's frustration and lack of action from her brother began to grow, it would seem that she had just swapped her reluctant father for a reluctant brother and any early promise Charles had shown in helping his sister's family seemed to be dwindling fast. In her mind, Charles was purposefully keeping Charles Louis and Rupert away from home so they could not negotiate with other factions but what the two brothers felt about their extended stay in England is unknown what we do know is that whilst they were at the Stuart court they were well treated and as the king's nephews they were lauded with extravagance and splendour. Regardless of what they thought, Charles had them in his grasp and was unwilling to let them go.

But what were his plans for his nephews? In January 1637 the king proposed that Charles Louis sail to the West Indies under the Palatinate flag but as part of an English fleet, he was sure to keep his direct involvement under wraps. Being even further away from Europe and any influence that there may have been at the English court would have been beneficial for Charles but Hesse was quick to point out to Elizabeth that Charles Louis would never recover his Palatinate lands by going on a naval expedition to the West Indies, he needed to be at home where he could launch further campaigns. Prince Rupert on the other hand was to lead an expedition to Madagascar with the intention of conquering the island and becoming its viceroy. Again, it was a ploy to remove him from Europe and as the second eldest brother he needed to be kept away lest he take up Charles Louis's cause. Neither of these wild plots came to fruition but what they did do was allow Charles Louis and Rupert believe their uncle was actively working on plans to help them regain the Palatinate, when in reality they were stalling tactics. The brothers were finally able to return to The Hague in June 1637 as it looked like Charles had at last secured his French alliance which meant he was finally able to declare open war against the Habsburg empire and Spain.

Emperor Ferdinand II died in early 1637 in Vienna at the age of 58. During his reign he had successfully led the Counter Reformation by reintroducing Catholicism across large parts of his empire showing religious intolerance towards Protestants. He was a dogmatic ruler and his behaviour led directly to the Bohemian Revolt. During his reign he also consolidated Habsburg power and enjoyed relative success on the battlefield but as with many opinions of the day your judgement was clouded by religion. To Catholics he was their defender and someone who ended their persecution whereas to the Protestants he was their oppressor who brought war to their towns and villages. He failed to bring any kind of unity to his empire, he was a competent but stern ruler whose actions had an impact of the Holy Roamn Empire and imperial rule.

With Ferdinand's death came an opportunity for Charles Louis to take up his role as Imperial Vicar as the Elector Palatine. However, the vote to elect the new King of the Romans, which was Charles Louis' by right was cast by Bavaria leading to the election of Ferdinand III who also became Emperor of the Holy Roman Empire following the death of his father, having been crowned King of Bohemia in 1627. This put King Charles in an awkward position for if he accepted the new king it would be a clear message that he was the rightful holder of the Palatinate Electoral dignity, which by rights fell to his nephew.

When Charles Louis and Rupert returned to the continent Elizabeth sent them to the Prince of Orange in Breda which at the time was under siege. The plan was for the brothers to gain valuable military experience whilst serving the Prince. Breda was finally liberated by the Dutch but such a great victory was over shadowed by the death of the Landgrave of Hesse on 10 October 1637. This death would have provided Charles Louis with an ideal opportunity to lead an army of his own from the front. The soldiers were keen to serve Charles Louis but the new leader, General Melander, refused to step aside. Elizabeth felt that her son fighting as a volunteer under the command of someone else would be a dishonour to him and his family, if he wanted the title of Elector then he had to be treated like one. What Charles Louis needed was an army of his own that he could lead from the front and his mother was about to provide him with one. For years money had been an issue for Elizabeth and Frederick but it seems she was actually sat on a fortune so she took a huge risk by taking all the money she had to buy her son an army. William, Baron Craven, generously gave £5,000 towards the cause and Elizabeth contributed the remaining £25,000 which, in total, would be approximately £3.5 million in today's money (Currency Converter, The National Archives) but that was the price to build a Palatine army from scratch.

The new garrison at Meppen swore loyalty to Charles Louis which encouraged King Charles to pledge a further £20,000 whilst the States General provided them with weapons and ammunition. The town of Meppen, which sits in present-day Lower Saxony, provided an annual revenue of approximately £10,000 so the monies raised to buy it would be repaid in several years. But as with many of Elizabeth's plans and hopes it was doomed to failure and Meppen was taken by the Emperor's forces on 1 May 1638. But not all hope was lost, the emperor may have secured the town but Charles Louis still had his band of loyal men and he was to unite them with the troops led by a Scottish Lieutenant-General serving in the Swedish army by the name of James King. King and a fellow commander called Alexander Leslie decided to keep their forces together for the use of Charles Louis. The armies merged together to fight for the Palatinate cause.

The plan was to converge on Lemgo a small town which was held by the Imperial Army, albeit weakly. If they were able to capture Lemgo it would give the Palatines a foothold in Germany and give them a sound base to launch further attacks and re-supply their men. Just prior to the attack at Lemgo, Charles Louis, Rupert and Craven, along with Rupert's men, led a reconnoitre of the imperially held town Rheine. The plan was to draw the enemy out from behind their walls and engage them in fighting before the defenders turned and retreated. Unfortunately, in his enthusiasm, Rupert drove his men on and as they charged at the enemy they failed to draw their pistols which resulted in an almighty crash which destroyed the enemies front line. In the excitement, Rupert and some of his men nearly got carried through the town's gates with the retreating army thankfully they didn't and they were quickly able to rejoin the main party. Here was an early sign that Rupert was going to live a soldiers life, he was a man that enjoyed combat and the thrill of a battle but it was also an indication he was at times uncontrollable in his charges, he proved to be recklessly wonderful in battle until the likes of Oliver Cromwell figured him out.

After they had arrived back at Lemgo they initially saw success and the town was soon under siege. However, it did not last long and the siege was soon lifted when the Imperial forces arrived and destroyed the combined Palatinate-Swedish forces. The defeated Palatine army needed a new plan and it was decided they would return to the safety of the Swedish Garrison at Minden to regroup so, on 16 October they set off. But the Imperial forces anticipated this move and managed to cut them off at Vlotho so when the weary Palatinate-Swedish army arrived they knew a battle was inevitable. No sooner had they lined up in formation they were set upon by the enemy, they broke through the first two lines of cavalry with ease but Rupert being Rupert was not willing to be a sitting duck, he charged at them with his men at his back. It worked, the imperialist forces retreated. But Rupert continued to charge and when he reached the bottom of the valley there was a fresh wave of soldiers waiting for him. But he had a plan and when he joined forces with Craven they both managed to force the army back down the valley into the open expanse where a great many men lost their lives.

Things did not go that well though and Rupert soon found himself isolated from his men but to his luck he was wearing a white cockade in his hat to which his men could rally to and it just so happened the imperial officers were wearing the same protecting him from attack. He could have escaped the battlefield undetected but he saw one of his own being attacked and went to his rescue thereby showing which side he was really on. Rupert's exhausted horse bolted and threw him to the ground; the opposition leader Colonel Lippe came across Rupert and ensured he had no way to escape. Charles Louis's army was utterly destroyed that day and Rupert would forever blame General King for the decisions he made for their downfall. As for Elizabeth, she had risked everything she had on her sons success but their inexperience had cost them dearly. The gamble failed spectacularly and she was left with very little money to live on which meant she was now wholly dependent on her brother and the Stuart allowance of £21,500 which she still continued to receive. The dire straits she saw herself in meant she could not risk offending Charles as it was within his power to remove her allowance and leave her destitute.

News soon filtered out that Prince Rupert had been captured and taken prisoner alongside Baron Craven, who had also suffered terrible injuries. William Craven, 1st Earl of Craven, was a loyal supporter of the Stuarts and one of England's wealthiest men and he spent much of his fortune in supporting Elizabeth and the Protestant cause across Europe. He would later go on to financially help Charles I during the Civil War and when his son was declared Charles II he accompanied the king back to England. Rupert, despite reports that he had been fatally wounded, was completely fine although his cloak had two bullet holes shot through it. Firstly, the prisoners were taken to Warrendorf where his keeper was an English colonel named Walter Devereaux. Rupert offered him all the money he had to let them escape, Devereaux declined but word got around and his jailer was changed. The prisoners were then taken to Bamberg where his fellow inmates, Ferentz and Craven, were ransomed for £20,000. Craven was so desperate to remain with Rupert that he offered to pay more than the ransom charge to stay alongside him, he even offered extortionate amounts for Rupert's freedom but there was no price high enough for that. It seems Craven's loyalty knew no bounds.

Finally, Rupert arrived at a castle in Linz a town that sits on the Danube in Austria. He would remain here for the next three years during which time he was kept under close surveillance and allowed no male company. The Emperor hoped to convert him to Catholicism and take him into his service. After much persuasion from King Charles, Cardinal Richelieu, and his own brother Archduke Leopold, the Emperor decide to slacken Rupert's imprisonment. He was allowed to visit nearby houses and even go riding, during a hunting trip Rupert shot a wild boar in front of the Emperor. His full release was quickly granted but he was to promise never to lead an army against the Emperor again. He travelled home via Vienna, Prague, Saxony and into Holland. He finally arrived back at The Hague where he was greeted by his mother.

The Stuart-Franco alliance was dealt a huge blow when the French took Charles Louis prisoner in October 1639. The capture was the accumulation of disasters Elizabeth faced at the end of the 1630s. She had wanted to place Charles Louis at the head of Bernard of Saxe-Wiemer's army. Rumours began to circulate that Bernard wished to marry the Princess Elisabeth which was a match her mother supported as Wiemer had been a long servant to the Protestant cause in the Thirty Years' War serving under Gustavus Adolphus. She dreamt of a grand marriage for her daughter but more importantly a grand army for her son. The marriage negotiations ended in July 1639 when Bernard died at the age of 34 due to poor health, he had been preparing for battle at the time of his death.

Elizabeth still had her eyes on the army and when the four military leaders swore to accept Charles Louis as their leader along with King Charles's support the Palatinate cause looked revived once more. Unfortunately, whilst on his way to meet his new troops at Breisach Charles Louis was apprehended by agents working for Cardinal Richelieu proving just how deceitful and double crossing the French were. Charles Louis was taken to Bois de Vincennes where he was imprisoned until

1640. Charles was quick to point out to his French counterpart that the kidnap of his nephew contravened the Anglo-French Alliance and until Charles Louis was released he would have nothing more to do with them. To the French however, the taking of Charles Louis meant they could take control of his newly found army but this proved to be a deeply unpopular move across Europe because as well as alienating the British it also irked the Danes and the Swedes.

Elizabeth's sons seemed to cause her no end of worry and when the youngest of her children, Gustavus Adolphus, died suddenly on 9 February 1641 at the age of just 8 years old she was heartbroken. The death brought about the end of the children's court at Leiden, which meant Princess Sophia was to relocate to The Hague to live with her mother. The Prinsenhof was returned to the city of Leiden with thanks for the seventeen years they had played host to her children.

Following his release, Charles Louis returned to England in February 1641 in an attempt to persuade parliament to support his cause. His arrival did not sit well with the king; he was struggling with a strong anti-Catholic movement that was sweeping the nation as well as having his own issues with Parliament. He was also a constant visual reminder that the young Palatine prince was a potential claimant to the three thrones currently inhabited by Charles I. The king made sure a close eye was kept on his nephew, he wanted to know his movements, who he saw and what was said, at this point Charles saw him as a genuine threat to his crown.

In 1641, the English and Scottish Parliaments both passed a manifesto that included the Palatinate cause, which was fantastic news for Charles Louis as it meant it was back on the negotiating table. Off the back of that, Charles vowed to take the upcoming Imperial Diet in Ratisbon (Regensberg) seriously. The Imperial Diet offered all member states and interested parties an opportunity to negotiate and discuss issues that were affecting the empire at any one particular time. The king clearly stated that if the Imperial Diet refused to restore Charles Louis by peaceful means then he would be left with no choice but to engage the Emperor in warfare. Naturally Elizabeth was over the moon at her brother's declaration, finally he had pinned his colours to one side and committed.

Prince Rupert, fresh from his release, quickly joined his elder brother in England but his stay was short as the king requested he accompany Queen Henrietta Mary and his daughter Mary, the Princess Royal, along with some items from the crown jewels, to The Hague for their own safety. Times were getting dangerous in England and rather than return with Rupert, Charles Louis accompanied his uncle to Newmarket.

Once the queen and her daughter were settled in The Hague, Elizabeth became her protector. And she soon set about helping her sister-in-law raise money for Charles by pawning some of the jewels the queen brought with her. With the help of the Prince of Orange the queen raised over £100,000 for the Stuart cause back in England where the relationship between uncle and nephew was slowly deteriorating. The king refused to forward any funds for Charles Louis's upkeep which meant he had to pawn his precious garter belt just to be able to continue to stay with the court. Things got worse in June 1642 when Charles refused to grant his nephew a fleet of ships to help crush the Irish rebellion that had been brewing for some time. To Charles Louis this showed a lack of trust from Charles and so in August, just after the start of the English Civil War, Charles Louis decided to return home to The Hague. Sailing in the opposite direction were his brothers Rupert and Maurice, who was now aged 21 years old, both of whom rallied to England's call for arms heading straight for the north where they joined the Royalist armies. Elizabeth had begged them not to travel but both were adamant they wanted to support their uncle. Maurice first saw battle at Powick Bridge just south of Worcester which proved to be a victory for the Royalist Army and just one month later on 23 October, they both fought at the Battle of Edgehill. Edgehill is considered to be the first major battle of the English Civil War, or, The War of Three Kingdoms as it is otherwise known. Numbers were fairly even; the Parliamentarian Army consisted of around 12,000 men and was led by Robert Devereux, 3rd Earl of Essex whilst the Royalists boasted 13,000. Under the command of the King, Rupert led the first charge which was successful to a point. The fighting was intense and both forces suffered losses with the total number of men being killed numbering roughly 1000 across both armies. The final outcome of the battle was inconclusive in that both sides suffered equal losses and even though both sides claimed victory neither won a decisive victory.

Thankfully both Rupert and Maurice survived the battle but Elizabeth and Charles Louis tried to distance themselves from the brothers and the events that were unfolding across the sea. In fact, it was Elizabeth that was named as a front runner to become the peacemaker by bringing Parliament and her brother together and many rumours went about that the king was making ready to receive his sister in Oxford, the base for his new court. On the other hand, the Parliamentarians were claiming she had ditched the royalist cause and had in fact sided with them, regardless of the fact two of her sons were fighting for the opposition. All of a sudden, whether she liked it or not, Elizabeth was mixed up with the events taking place in England and her sons involvement in the war hit her finances hard when her pension was stopped by parliament. She had remained popular in England but she could not be persuaded to act as a mediator on either side, maybe if she had, England would have been saved much bloodshed but she had other problems to deal with.

To Elizabeth's mind, Rupert and Maurice should be fighting on German soil in a bid to win back the Palatinate for their brother but as they continued to enjoy success on the English battlefields the likelihood of them returning was a distant dream. His impressive wins on the battlefield meant that at the age of 22, Maurice became the youngest member of King Charles's Council of War. In August 1644, Charles Louis returned to England much to the anger of Parliament but he was there to drum up support for his own battles and not to join his brothers fighting for the king. Parliament had other pressing matters to deal with than supporting a war on foreign soil, they had war on their own doorstep and the last thing they needed was another Palatine brother involving themselves in England's war.

With her three eldest sons engaged elsewhere it was the turn of Prince Edward to stir up trouble for Elizabeth when he decided to marry without the consent of his mother or Charles Louis. He had met and fallen in love with Anne de Gonzaga of the house of Nevers, she was sister to the Queen of Poland and the daughter of Carol I, Duke of Mantua and of French and Italian descent. The couple married on 24 April 1645 in Paris but the most shocking aspect of the marriage was that in order to have the marriage recognised in France, Edward had to convert to Catholicism. Unlike his elder brothers the soldiers life was not for Edward, usually a younger son would enter the church but it was clear he was content to live a life of excess in the Parisian salons frequented by his wife. For Anna it was quite an achievement to have captured a man of Edward's rank and it cemented her place at the heart of Parisian society. The couple took the title of Prince and Princess of Palatine and enjoyed all the trappings that came with a royal title. News of the marriage and Edward's conversion knocked Elizabeth off her feet and both Charles Louis and Princess Elisabeth chastised their brother over what they saw as a betrayal especially as it had led to Pope Innocent XI and Holy Roman Emperor to believe he would have been a good candidate to become the next Elector Palatine. Could this be the catalyst that shifted the power back to Elizabeth's family? Their mother did relent but it took time but she did send the newlyweds a set of tapestries as a wedding gift. His mother's acceptance and forgiveness was not what Edward expected given she had previously said she 'would rather strangle my children with my own hands' than see them convert to Catholicism.

On 2 July 1644, Rupert tasted defeat at the Battle of Marston Moor. Along with Edgehill this was one of the most significant and largest battles of the English Civil War and the Parliamentarian win had a big impact on Royalist power in the North. Rupert was in command of the king's forces and the disaster that unfolded in Yorkshire was planted firmly at his feet. He underestimated the strength and will to engage in battle of the enemy, a combined force of Scottish and Parliamentarian troops. He assumed they would retreat or delay entering the battlefield but their combined number of men totalled 27,000 which outnumbered the Royalists by 10,000. Rupert's positioning was also called into question when he chose to place his men on lower ground whilst the enemy took a position higher up on the moor giving them a clear tactical advantage. Despite some success on the right flank Rupert failed to regroup and shift to support the centre and left flank. As a result, Oliver Cromwell's men drove straight through the Royalist ranks which decimated the army. The king's army lost over 4,000 men and soon after the pivotal city of York also fell. Rupert's reputation took a hammering following this rout and he was accused of being arrogant which had led to him being a liability to his men. To compound his misery, he saw his faithful poodle, Boy, killed. Allegedly Rupert had been forced to flee the battle and take refuge in a nearby bean field. This was a significant defeat as it led the Parliamentarian forces taking control of much of northern England.

Good news arrived for Elizabeth in March 1645 when her pension allowance was reinstated thanks to a petition by her one-time loyal friend and now Parliamentarian supporter the Earl of Essex, however, the payments remained sporadic and at varying amounts. When the 1645 fighting season began the Parliamentarian forces reconvened under Oliver Cromwell, Thomas Fairfax and their New Model Army whilst Rupert was appointed the Captain-General of the King's Forces. Things did not get off to a great start for Rupert when the Royalist Army suffered a huge defeat at the Battle of Naseby on 14 June 1645. The Battle of Naseby was another of the so-called big battles of the English Civil War and one which saw the annihilation of the Royalist army, led once again by Prince Rupert. Like at Marston Moor, the Parliamentarian New Model Army took a position on the higher ground after Cromwell noticed the ground between armies was marshy and this movement of the opposition forced Rupert to begin his attack. He successfully broke through the enemies left flank but rather than turn his men back to and launch a further attack on the remaining army he forced them on in pursuit of the cavalry which he overwhelmed. But this error gave Cromwell an opportunity to carry out a successful attack against the royalist infantry and left flank. It was clear Cromwell was going to be victorious and many of the royalist troops surrendered and by the time Rupert and his cavalry returned to the battlefield all was lost. This defeat marked the loss of the south and west areas of England and less than a year later King Charles I had surrendered.

Rupert was no fool and he could see there was no point in the King continuing the fight. The Parliamentarians held all the cards and Rupert urged his uncle to come to terms with his enemies but Charles refused and dismissed Rupert and Maurice from their duties. Rumours did the rounds that Rupert had his eyes on the crown which no doubt led Charles to make such a decision but there was never ever evidence to support this claim and when he stood accused of treason at a court-martial hearing he was cleared of all charges leading the king to reconcile with his nephews.

King Charles travelled to Scotland in a last ditched attempt to win over the Scottish government but the Covenanters took him prisoner, however, they still allowed him to hold secret discussions with his sympathisers. Rupert was not happy to hear that the King had entered into negotiations with the Covenanters and decided to remain in Oxford until 1646 when the town surrendered to Parliamentarians. Thankfully Rupert and Maurice were given passes to leave the country safely but technically as they were not English citizens the parliamentarians may not have held any jurisdiction over them. Rupert decided to go to France to visit his brother Edward and Maurice returned home to The Hague. Having two sons fight in an English army was forgivable but to have a son that had converted to Catholicism and marry without consent took a little longer to forgive but Elizabeth's second youngest son Philip Frederick was about to blow them all out of the water with his behaviour when he murdered her close friend and servant Jacques d'Espinay, Lord of Vaux, Geraux and Mezieres.

Elizabeth had appointed d'Espinay as her Master of the Horse in 1645 but court gossip soon followed that he had formed an intimate relationship with Elizabeth and her daughter Louise Hollandine. The rumour mill went into overdrive and even claimed that the young princess had given birth to his child in Leiden. Given that Philip Frederick was the eldest son still left at home in The Hague he took it upon himself to defend the honour of his mother and sister. Philip Frederick ordered d'Espinay to leave court but the Frenchman chose to ignore the threat as he had Elizabeth's invitation to visit and he felt that held more sway. Later that evening Philip Frederick was attacked on his way home but was able to positively identify d'Espinay as one of his assailants. Hell bent on revenge, the following day Philip Frederick, accompanied several of his men, spotted d'Espinay whilst he was walking to his lodgings, they gave chase and caught up with him at the Market Square where they attacked him with their knives. D'Espinay died from his injuries later that day. Philip Frederick was easy to identify given the bright red trousers he had chosen to wear that day and he, along with the rest of the group, were summoned to court but it was too late, they had already fled meaning no verdict could be passed against them.

Philip Frederick first fled to Cleves and then onto Brussels but he was a wanted man, the French were determined to catch him and have their revenge. It appeared he was an impatient and hot-headed young man who was desperate to be on the battlefields alongside his elder brothers. But for Elizabth, her impetuous younger son had gone too far, Charles Louis pleaded with his mother to forgive him given his tender age of 17 and also because he was her flesh and blood, to his mind it didn't matter the crime you forgave your family. Even Princess Elisabeth tried to intercede on her brother's behalf. She had been in communication with French philosopher Rene Descartes about how passions can inform a person's behaviour but even that held no sway with Elizabeth and led to her falling out with her daughter too. It seems Elizabeth was at war with most of her children and so after feeling the force of her mother's wrath Elisabeth went into a self-imposed exile at the Brandenberg courts at Berlin and Crossen.

Over in England the news was not any better. Charles had been taken prisoner by Parliamentarian forces in January 1647 but that did not stop the war that had ripped England apart. The Royalist army rose again in May 1648 but a crushing defeat at the Battle of Preston all but sealed the king's fate. The Prince of Wales, Charles Stuart, and his younger brother James, Duke of York had managed to escape to the Dutch Republic and the safety of their aunt Elizabeth's court. Elizabeth enjoyed her nephews company and would often visit the theatre with Charles, unbeknownst to them what was unfolding across the sea in England. King Charles I was put on trial and found guilty of treason, a crime that is punishable by death and being a king did not alter the punishment. On Tuesday 30 January 1649, King Charles I of England, Scotland and Ireland stepped through the window of the Banqueting House in Whitehall onto a purpose-built scaffold. It is said he requested two shirts to wear that morning has he didn't want the cold weather to make him shiver making him look weak and frightened. Once on the scaffold he addressed the public that had gathered to witness such a monumental event. He declared he wanted freedom for his people and concluded with 'I shall go from a corruptible to an incorruptible crown, where no disturbance can be'. At 2pm the king lay his head on the block, stretched his arms out and waited for the blow of the axe. The executioner beheaded the king with one single blow of the axe. The assembled crowd let out a collective groan, the realisation of what had just taken place shocking them into near silence, some even dipped their handkerchiefs into the king's blood as a memento. He had become a martyr to the royalists and members of the Anglican Church as he died defending the divine right of kings and that was a role appointed by God. The very fact that he refused to compromise and come to terms with his enemies showed his dedication to his religious principles and that was appreciated and recognised those in the Anglican Church. Like all things there is always a flip side and to the Parliamentarians and Puritans, King Charles I was nothing but a tyrant who abused his power by plunging the country into Civil War. When the news reached The Hague, Elizabeth, the king's sister and Mary his daughter screamed in despair, their grief and heartbreak clear for all to see. The unthinkable had happened.

Part VI

1649–1662

The execution of Charles I brought his son to the throne as King Charles II but as a monarch in exile it brought many of his supporters to The Hague. Elizabeth, who had plenty of experience in living as an exiled monarch, supported her nephew in his plans to regain his birthright, but patience, as always, would be the key. On 25 June 1649 Charles left The Hague and joined his mother in France, his sister Mary of Orange and Elizabeth accompanied him part of the way. Following the king's execution Rupert and Maurice landed in Ireland and set up camp in Kinsale, a town on the river Bandon in County Cork. From there, their fleet of 28 ships were able to patrol the southern coast of England. Parliament were concerned and so sent their main fleet under the command of Robert Blake to blockade the town giving Cromwell's men the opportunity to land and progress through Ireland. Rupert and Maurice managed to escape to Portugal with just seven of their remaining ships.

In early 1649, Charles Louis signed the Peace of Westphalia which saw a partial restoration of the Lower Palatinate but Bavaria still held the power and rights of the electorate, it was a positive step forward in the eyes of Charles Louis. The seven electors agreed to create an eighth electorate for Charles Louis but this did not restore his father's powers or title of Elector Palatine, that too went to Bavaria. Elizabeth was not happy at what she felt was an abandonment of Charles Louis's princely status as well as the lucrative Upper Palatinate lands. But to Charles Louis, it was more than his parents had ever managed to regain and he was happy with his lot. He was practical and understood it was highly unlikely he would ever receive the military support needed to fully restore his father's lands and titles so made the best of what was on offer and this meant a return to Heidelberg.

The death of her brother at the hands of the Parliamentarians put an end to any hope Elizabeth had of regaining her pensions, instead she switched to the States General in the hope they would offer her some financial support. Lucky for Elizabeth they were happy to help but stopped short at offering her a full pension and soon her debts were spiralling out of control. She had a court of around eighty individuals who all had to be fed and lodged. Since she paid for Charles Louis's disastrous campaigns this had become a burden she could no longer afford and she was advised to halve the numbers. A request was sent to England for £2660 to be forwarded for Elizabeth's personal use but also for them to clear her debts which totalled around £15,000, most of which she owed to merchants in The Hague. Naturally the English refused so the States General changed tack and asked them to provide the back payments that were owed on her pension which, on the face of it, is not an unreasonable request. All appeared to be working until Prince Edward interfered and called the Parliament's ambassadors in The Hague, Walter Strickland and Oliver St John, rogues and dogs. His arrogance knew no bounds and as a prince of the Palatinate he felt had done well to speak of the English like this but his behaviour concerned Elizabeth who was worried the States General would abandon her altogether because of his ill-judged comments. To fan the flames Elizabeth sent Edward to Germany as news filtered through that Frankenthal had been restored to Charles Louis and she wanted it back.

Further good news came when on 4 April 1651 Princess Henriette Marie married Sigismund Rákóczi, brother of George Rákóczi II, Prince of Transylvania in Hungary. Sadly, the happiness was not to last as Henriette Marie died unexpectedly just five months later on 18 September. Her husband died not long after and both were buried in St Michael's Cathedral in Alba Iulia, Romania.

Henriette Maries's death is not the only one Elizabeth would mourn. Philip Frederick was serving in the army under the Duke of Lorraine with the rank of Colonel when he was killed at the age of 23 at the Battle of Rethel in France on 6 December 1650. He had never returned to The Hague to answer the charges against him and so enlisted to fight for

France in the Fronde (a time of civil unrest during the minority reign of Louis XIV) and the wider Franco-Spanish War. He was buried in Sedan in the Ardennes region of France in the Church of St Charles Borromeo. He had become the very thing Elizabeth had sworn none of her sons would be – a soldier of fortune. There is no record of Elizabeth's reaction to her son's death but when his sister Princess Elisabeth heard the news she was unable to sleep for several days as she could not shake the image of her brother from her mind.

Relations between Charles Louis and his mother were continuing to deteriorate and when he suggested she stopped using the title of Queen of Bohemia she was extremely insulted. She explained to her son that the title meant more to her than grandeur, it was an honour to her late husband who gave her the title, and she hoped maybe one day she might regain it. It also gave her children the right to Palatinate lands so it wasn't just a case of Elizabeth being vain, this was a mother protecting her children's birthrights. But in Charles Louis's view now he had regained the Lower Palatine and the rest had gone to Bavaria he felt there was no need for her to continue using the title, especially as it caused offence to the Emperor. Charles Louis needed to be mindful over the requests he made of people because by asking his mother to desist in using her title he was in effect calling his father a usurper and that kind of behaviour was not welcome by anyone.

Elizabeth was beginning to feel unwelcome in The Hague. The States General had warned her nephew the Duke of York to make sure his court was kept in order, but worse than that, they were also in open negotiations with her enemies, the English and in 1652 the first Anglo-Dutch trade war broke out. It saw many of the Stuart supporters leave The Hague for Germany and saw the start of Elizabeth's influence waning. Meanwhile Rupert and Maurice were sailing along the west African coast where they captured an English ship which Maurice renamed 'Defiance' and of which he made himself the vice-admiral. From Africa they sailed to the West Indies where in September 1652 they encountered a storm. Rupert's ship survived but 'Defiance' was lost off the coast of the Virgin Islands. Maurice went down with his ship but was not officially declared dead until 1664. Elizabeth hoped her son had managed to get to shore and was perhaps being held prisoner by the Spanish but in reality and deep down she knew that Maurice became the second son she had lost to drowning. The loss to the family was deeply felt, Rupert was devastated by his brother's death, the two had been close in more than age and he felt responsible for his younger brother's welfare. Maurice had been a vocal supporter of his elder brother throughout their military exploits across England and Ireland, when things went wrong Rupert was guaranteed to have Maurice stand shoulder to shoulder with him. Edward returned to The Hague when he heard the news of his brother's drowning to offer comfort to his mother and sister Louise Hollandine. After losing two sons in quick succession and Frederick Henry, Gustavus Adolphus and Louis years before, it is understandable why she was happy to forgive Edward as readily as she did. But the Edward that returned home from Paris was a confident man now a husband and father and no doubt he was happy to present his daughters to their grandmother.

Elizabeth had been harbouring hopes of moving back to Frankenthal and was disappointed to learn it was not fit to be lived in so she instead looked towards her marital home of Heidelberg Castle. She was ready to leave The Hague and since returning to England was not an option at that time, the issue she faced was her son. Charles Louis had no intention of reinstating her marriage jointure as he needed the revenue to rebuild his fortunes and it was from this point we see him step back from claiming any responsibility for his mother's upkeep. He refused to contribute towards her debts that now stood totalling approximately £93,000 (approximately £9.5 million in today's money). The States of Holland were willing to pay nearly £20,000 off the debt if Elizabeth was willing to pawn her jewellery and plate, the States General would then advance her a payment of £15,000. Charles Louis's reluctance to help settle his mother's financial burdens smarted all the more for Elizabeth given she had practically bankrupted herself to help Charles Louis to regain what was rightfully his. It also became apparent that he had been withholding assets that legally belonged to his mother and in a bizarre turn of events it was the Emperor that stepped forward to offer Elizabeth help.

He was offering her a sum of money that Charles Louis had purposely kept from her for himself. Elizabeth was desperate, the English refused to help, her son was adamant she would get nothing from him and declared her title was invalid in Germany and she would never accept help from her enemies so in the end she had to remain in The Hague.

In 1654, the States of Holland granted Elizabeth a pension of £1,200 per annum but she still needed more and regardless of the repeated knock backs she continued to petition her son to help her but each time he declined stating his funds were going towards the rebuilding of Heidelberg and that his mother was not a priority. Was more going on behind the scenes with Charles Louis? Perhaps there was. In 1650 he had married Charlotte of Hesse, daughter of Wilhelm V and Amalie Elisabeth, Landgrave and Landgravine of Hesse, The couple had three children together, two of which reached adulthood including his heir, the future Elector Palatine, Charles II, and a younger daughter called Elizabeth Charlotte, Madame Palatine. The marriage was doomed from the start; Charlotte was a constant nagging thorn in Charles Louis side whilst she found her husband cold and stand offish. So, it came as no surprise after seven years of marriage Charles Louis petitioned for divorce on the account he had fallen in love with one of his wife's ladies-in-waiting, Baroness Louise von Degenfeld. Louise had been born in November 1634 in Strasbourg to a penniless German Baron called Christoph Martin von Degenfeld and his wife Maria Anna Adelmann von Adelmannsfelden. She was appointed as a lady-in-waiting to Charlotte shortly after her marriage to Charles Louis in 1650.

Charles Louis wrote many love letters to his new amore begging her to become his mistress but she declined wanting to protect her honour but that did nothing but spur Charles Louis on, and he resolved to make her his wife. Unfortunately for him, Charlotte had no intention of granting him a divorce. In fact, when she became aware of her husband's infidelity she resolved to make life extremely difficult for him, she would not allow them to meet, let alone become married. Things became even more complicated during a stay in Heidelberg. Rupert, who had a low opinion of his elder brother, also fell under the charm of Louise. He left a note for her saying that he had become infatuated with her, Louise found the note but believed it to be for Charlotte and so passed it on to her. It then all became a bit of a farce especially when Charlotte confronted Rupert about the note causing her huge embarrassment when she realised it was not for her but for her rival Louise, who she then accused of being nothing short of a whore.

Just a few nights following this debacle Charlotte came across her husband in bed with Louise and her anger spilled over and she attacked her husband's lover by biting her hard on the little finger, it could have been much worse had Charles Louis not been there to call the guards to separate his wife and lover. This episode was not even the lowest depth Charlotte sank to because when she found a bundle of love letters and jewels that had passed between the two lovers, she confronted Louise. She screamed and shouted and hurled abuse as her whilst she cowered behind Charles Louis. During this row Princess Elisabeth, who was staying with her brother at the time, walked in but she just began to laugh at the absurd situation she saw unfolding before her eyes. Charlotte then began to laugh hysterically and she threw the jewels back at Louise after Charles Louis requested she give them back. Things had clearly got to a worrying level; Charles Louis was seriously concerned for the welfare of Louise and so had her apartments moved to those directly above his. This convenient location meant the two lovers had easy access to one another, especially after Charles Louis had a hole cut in the ceiling so he could place a ladder up to her room. When Charlotte discovered the secret meeting places she climbed the ladder with a knife in her hand intent on who knows what. Thankfully her ladies managed to restrain her before she committed an act of violence that would result in her own destruction. Charles Louis officially separated from Charlotte and contracted a morganatic marriage (and a bigamous one) to Louise von Degenfeld on 6 January 1658 at Schwetzingen Castle. The couple would have thirteen children together and given the situation those children could never lay claim to Charles Louis's titles, land or wealth. She took on the title of raugräfin meaning a countess with no land, their children became known as Raugraves/Raugravine. Out of the thirteen children only one married and had children of their own and that was their daughter Raugravine Caroline Elisabeth who married Meinhard, 3rd Duke of Schomberg and 1st Duke of Leinster in 1683. Tragically three of their sons would die in battle whilst another was killed after losing a duel and their youngest died unmarried and an alcoholic in 1702. Of the thirteen, five did not reach adulthood and the remaining daughters, for whatever reasons remained unmarried. Sadly, Louise would die during her fourteenth pregnancy on 18 March 1677 at Friedrichsburg Castle in Mannheim. She had given birth near enough once a year throughout her marriage, she was 42 years old. The marriage between Charles Louis and Louise was for the most part a happy one but there were times, especially in the earlier years when they remained under the same roof as Charlotte, that quarrels happened. He managed to have Charlotte returned to her family in Hesse for a time which led to a happy homelife for Charles Louis and his children. His two children by Charlotte by and large got on well with their half-siblings and their step-mother.

But what became of Charlotte? As far as she was concerned she wasn't going to give up her lifestyle so easily. She moved into a wing at Heidelberg in the hope the decision made regarding her marriage being annulled could be reversed and Charles Louis would return to her. Her daughter Elisabeth Charlotte was sent by Charles Louis to live with his sister Sophia in Hanover. We are not fully aware of what Charlotte's relationship was like with her two children but it was clear Charles Louis did not want his daughter to be influenced by her mother in any way. On the other hand, he could have been sparing his young daughter the pain of her parents broken marriage and spending time at the Hanoverian court would have provided her with an invaluable education in courtly life. He was a loving and doting father to all of his children, although as Charles grew older the relationship between the father and his heir became strained.

Sophia despised her sister-in-law finding her vain and stupid and full of anger. Her character appears to have been unstable and erratic and more worryingly she appears unable to control her rages and so she was more than happy to take her niece into her care. Whilst Sophia did not get along with Charlotte, her other sister-in-law, Elisabeth openly supported her and defied her brother by doing so. When Charlotte finally left Heidelberg in June 1663, Elizabeth Charlotte was permitted to return to the Palatine court. When Louise died in 1677, Charlotte still remained adamant she would not grant Charles Louis a divorce so he could remarry and gain another heir. His eldest son by Charlotte, Prince Charles had been unhappily married for seven years and had remained childless by his wife, Princess Wilhelmina Ernestine of Denmark. With no other option Charles Louis married for a third time in the hope Charlotte would divorce him to allow him to gain another legitimate heir for the Palatine. He married Elisabeth Hollander von Bernau, daughter of Tobias Hollander von Berau, on 11 December 1679 and the couple had one child, a son named Charles Louis in April 1681, sadly Charles Louis died not knowing his wife was pregnant as he died just one month after the baby was conceived. Charlotte refused to grant her husband's wishes and the infant Charles Louis remained, in the eyes of the law, a child by a morganatic marriage and unable to inherit any of his father's titles or wealth. In the end it was irrelevant as sadly the little boy would die at a young age. When Charles Louis died in 1680 Charlotte returned to Heidelberg at the request of her son Charles II and to the title of Dowager Electress Palatine, she died there on 26 March 1686 at the age of 58. But what are we to make of Charlotte's behaviour towards Charles Louis? At times she seemed unhinged and very dangerous, she definitely saw herself as a woman scorned in love but considering she didn't even want to marry Charles Louis you would have assumed she had jumped at the chance of a divorce. On the other hand, she may have been worried that by divorcing him she would have lost all access to her children, which she pretty much did anyway but her reputation as a divorced woman could have impacted her future hopes of remarrying. On balance though she does seemed to have caused Charles Louis unnecessary hurt, he appears to have been reasonable in his early actions but once it became clear to all that their marriage was over perhaps Charlotte should have reached a settlement that benefitted her.

Elizabeth kept out of her son's private life, as a man he was free to do as he pleased but the same could not be said for her daughters, and one in particular was about to cut herself off from her mother permanently. Louise Hollandine left The Hague in the dead of night and headed for the southern Netherlands to take Holy Communion. She had converted to Catholicism and in order to save her mother the distress of her receiving the sacrament in her residence she decided the best thing to do was to leave. She was aided in her escape by her friend Maria Elisabeth II, Marquise of Bergen-op-Zoom and letters found in the princesses room told of a plot to deceive Elizabeth. The plan was to tell her mother that her brother Edward needed her in Paris but instead she was to travel to Antwerp in Maria Elisabeth's carriage and from there head to France.

Unfortunately, Louise Hollandine failed to destroy or take the letters with her when she left and they were found by Elizabeth the following day. It was all she needed as evidence to take to the States General to show that there had been plotting against her, she wanted her daughter arrested and returned to her. For her trouble Maria Elisabeth was temporarily stripped of her title and power. She craved an audience with Elizabeth as she wished to explain that actually Louise Hollandine was seven months pregnant, was being pregnant whilst unmarried a lesser scandal than converting to Catholicism? Maria Elisabeth was hoping Elizabeth would think so but she refused to see her, the betrayal was too much to bear. Louise Hollandine officially converted to Catholicism in an English Carmelite House on 25 January 1658. It would seem that one by one each of Elizabeth's children were turning away from her and the breakdown in the relationship with her daughter caused a lifetime of resentment. Louise Hollandine settled at Queen Henrietta Maria's convent the Visitation of Sainte Marie de Chaillot on the outskirts of Paris. Henrietta Maria, along with her brother Louis XIV and his wife Anne of Austria, tried to intervene with Elizabeth on Louise Hollandine's behalf but she was a stubborn woman who would not tolerate this behaviour. She did however relent and supposedly forgave her daughter but Louise Hollandine was the only surviving child to be omitted from her mother's Will. In September 1660 Louise Hollandine became a nun at the Cistercian Maubuisson Abbey where in August 1664 she became Abbess.

On 3 September 1658, Oliver Cromwell died at Westminster meaning the fortunes of the Stuarts were on the rise again. Cromwell nominated his son Richard as his heir but he lacked the authority and political acumen of his father and he quickly resigned his post, leaving Britain on the precipice of change. This news brought Elizabeth great joy and before long she was planning her long-awaited return to England but at around the same time her health began to show signs of decline. By May 1660, King Charles II had been invited by Parliament to take up the thrones of England, Scotland and Ireland. The news was celebrated in The Hague, not only was Elizabeth the aunt of the king but all her debts were finally settled by Parliament meaning she was free to return to England when Charles called for her. Unfortunately, the call did not come and to compound the misery further, Elizabeth had to mourn the loss of her young nephew the Henry, Duke of Gloucester who died aged 20 at the Palace of Whitehall from smallpox. Henry had accompanied his elder brothers back to England and was preparing for the coronation when he was struck down by the illness that would also claim the life of his sister Mary the Dowager Princess of Orange. They are buried beside each other in Westminster Abbey.

At the age of 64 and after spending forty-nine years living on the continent Elizabeth Stuart, Queen of Bohemia and Dowager Electress of the Palatine was ready to go home. Her daughter Sophia and her husband Ernst Augustus, Duke of Brunswick-Lüneburg came to bid her farewell. In a revealing letter to Prince Rupert, Elizabeth confesses Charles had asked her to remain in The Hague until further notice but seeing as she had already packed her bags and said her goodbyes she continued on her journey, the letter had arrived too late. She arrived a Gravesend on 26 May 1660 so it was no wonder the king was not thrilled to see his aunt when she arrived in London. He refused to grant her a set of apartments at court in Whitehall, instead she went to stay with her old friend Lord Craven on Drury Lane before settling at Leicester House.

Elizabeth Stuart died on 13 February 1662 at Leicester House, London aged 65. Following her death her embalmed body was placed into a coffin covered with black velvet before being transferred to Somerset

House where she lay in state for a day. From there her body was taken by river to Westminster Abbey for the funeral service, after which she was laid to rest in the Henry VII Lady Chapel next to her beloved brother Henry Frederick. Elizabeth lost much in her life, her husband, children, land and titles but she never lost the love of the English people, she was their Queen of Hearts and they mourned her loss deeply. Charles Louis inherited his mother's estates whilst her favourite son Rupert got her rings and plate. Edward received a diamond whilst Elisabeth inherited a pair of emerald earrings and the youngest surviving child Sophia received a pearl necklace. Louise Hollandine received nothing. It would be through her daughter Sophia that Elizabeth's legacy grew. Sophia's son George Ludwig, Elector of Hanover would become King George I when he inherited the British throne in 1714 meaning Elizabeth Stuart's blood runs down the royal line to our current monarch, King Charles III. But what of her other surviving children and grandchildren, would they leave their marks on Europe as she had?

The Children,
1662–1714

The year was 1662. King Charles II sits on the throne of England, and Elizabeth Stuart is dead. She outlived seven of her children and her husband, living a life of politics and intrigue. The baby Prince Louis was the first of the Palatine children to die at just 4 months old. Still, perhaps the biggest loss Elizabeth and Frederick faced was the drowning of their eldest son and heir, Frederick Henry, he had embodied their hopes for the future of the Palatinate. He drowned in 1629, devastating the couple; many believe this loss broke Frederick's health. Princess Charlotte followed her brothers to an early grave in January 1632 at the age of just 2 years old. Elizabeth was left reeling further when Frederick died just eleven months after his young daughter and Gustavus Adolphus, the youngest of Elizabeth's sons, died on 11 January 1641 at the tender age of 8. Then, heartbreak struck again when Elizabeth lost three of her children in three years. The first death came in December 1650 when the rogue Philip Frederick died whilst fighting for France and just less than a year his newly married sister Henriette Marie died in September 1651. Then came the loss of Maurice in September 1652 when he drowned off the coast of the West Indies, although he was not officially declared dead until 1664, Elizabeth always harboured dreams that he might have somehow survived, sadly, he didn't.

To suffer the death of one child is heartbreaking, but to lose seven, of all but one, of whom survived early babyhood and even reached adulthood in some cases, is truly devastating. Elizabeth has often been called a heartless, cold and uninterested mother, but I feel we must judge her by the standards of her day and not ours. We must also remember that a woman of her rank would not have been a 'hands-on' parent when it came to bringing her children up. One thing we can say for certain though is that she educated them well, the sons in warfare and the daughters in languages and classics, no one can accuse Elizabeth Stuart of not readying her children for a future in elevated circles.

As Elizabeth was laid to rest, her surviving children Charles Louis, Elisabeth, Rupert, Louise Hollandine, Edward and Sophia faced their futures without their indomitable mother to turn to. Not all of the surviving Palatine Princes and Princesses would lead fulfilling lives; some would die relatively soon after their mother, whilst others would go on to be remembered as pivotal people in the history of the continent and at home in Great Britain.

Charles Louis, Elector Palatine

Elizabeth and Frederick's eldest surviving son Charles Louis was not born to rule. As the second son he was the spare to the heir Frederick Henry but when his elder brother drowned in 1629 at the age of 15 it catapulted Charles Louis to first in line to the succession of the Palatinate lands. Unfortunately, Charles Louis and his family were living in exile in The Hague when his father died prematurely at the age of 36 in November 1632. The nearly 15-year-old Charles Louis not only became the head of the family but he also took on the responsibility of trying to regain his father's lands and territories.

He looked towards England in a bid to help his achieve his aims despite the country teetering on the edge of civil war and between 1635 and 1642 he spent approximately two and half years in his uncle's realms. Charles Louis decided to visit his uncle, Charles I on the advice of his mother and during his stay he visited Scotland where he sat in their government, an act that secured a promise of 10,000 Scottish Covenanter soldiers for the Palatine cause. The plan was they would follow their new leader back to Germany to engage in warfare under his banner but the outbreak of the Irish Rebellion saw them deployed across the Irish Sea in a bid to protect the Protestant cause.

The relationship between nephew and uncle began to grow more strained. The king believed Charles Louis could become a beacon for the parliamentarians who would seek to place him on the throne. It didn't help matters that Charles Louis held sympathetic parliamentarian views as he believed they would be more inclined to support his Palatine cause. Soon the two kinsmen became estranged and Charles I never trusted his nephew again. Charles Louis left England and returned to his mother in The Hague, his next visit back to England would not be until 1644 at a time when England was at war with itself.

His arrival at Gravesend on 29 August 1644 was met with suspicion on both sides and it appears he had come uninvited leading the king to ask him, 'upon what invitation you are come?' Originally Parliament had intended to allow him to stay for just two weeks but after a committee was sent to delegate with him on 31st they found him in support of theirs, and not the royalist cause so he was given dispensation to stay for longer, he would in fact stay for five years. He tried to promote himself as a neutral for he needed the king's influence on the continent. Charles Louis arrival is noted in the House of Lords Journal as thus,

> "That the Parliament did not know of his Electoral Highness' Arrival, or of any Intention of his coming into this Kingdom, till Twelve a Clock on Thursday last.
>
> "That, considering the Conjuncture of Affairs both at Home and Abroad, the Parliament is much surprized by not being informed and consulted with before his coming over; and doth conceive that the Residence of his Electoral Highness at this Time in Foreign Parts will be of more Advantage to his own and the Public Interest.
>
> "The Parliament hath always been most tender of his Electoral Highness' Affairs, is so, and will be; and have now sent a Committee of their own to visit him, and to give Assurance thereof, which they will ever express in their Actions and faithful Advice."

It would appear from this that any rumours that it was Parliament that invited him were unfounded as they clearly had no idea he was coming. The king was still very wary of his nephew, believing he had come to usurp his throne with Parliaments help when in fact all he really wanted was peace in England and assistance for the Palatinate. But his disloyalty towards the royalist cause, and his own family, led Charles I to form a distrust of Rupert who he decided to dismiss from his military post following his surrender at Bristol in September 1645, it would seem the king thought the Palatinate brothers were in cahoots with each other to claim his crown.

It was common knowledge that Parliament held the purse strings and that the king had no influence over who monetary awards could be made to. Charles Louis, aware of this and the financial burdens he and his family were under decided it best to side with the wealthier of the two sides, it seems family loyalty came at too high of a price. This was a point that clearly rankled the king as he accused Charles Louis of siding with his enemies for financial gain only and to better his own cause, the very fact that his nephew had seemly put a price on his loyalty led to king to part ways with Charles Louis. But in reality what option did Charles Louis have? As an exiled ruler leading an impoverished existence he had to grease the palms of those who could help, he could not afford the price of family loyalty and neither could he fight without an army. Charles would have taken the same line had he been in a similar situation, as I mentioned earlier in relation to King James, the nation comes before family and you are a lucky ruler if you can satisfy both.

Charles Louis let the neutrality mask slip when he agreed to the terms of the Solemn League and Covenant. This was a treaty that sought to preserve the reformed religion in Scotland, the reformation in England and Ireland with the expulsion of the Catholic Church. This was an agreement which was not necessarily something the royalists agreed with, putting Charles Louis in direct conflict with the king and his younger brothers Rupert and Maurice who both served as generals in the royalist army. Charles Louis saw an opportunity to capitalise on the unity between Scotland and the English parliament. Many of the Covenanters had talked up the Palatine cause and made no secret of the fact they had actively tried to find troops and build military bases. Parliament insisted that Charles I lend his support to the Palatine which led Charles Louis to believe a reconciliation between the King and his government was on the horizon and that in order for him to be restored on the continent peace in England was vital.

But all his pandering to Parliament did nothing to repair the fractured relationship between uncle and nephew. The pair met for the last time in 1647 and it was at this meeting the king accused Charles Louis of betrayal and for coveting his crown. On 24 October 1648, The Peace of Westphalia was agreed upon which brought to an end the Thirty Years' War and partially restored Charles Louis to his lands and estates in the

Lower Palatine. He was also given a new eighth Electoral Vote which restored to him some of the power his father had lost. Had he been on the continent during discussions he may have negotiated a better deal for himself rather than being involved in English affairs, at least that was the view of his mother and to be fair she had a point. The fact was he had no representation at the talks at all which meant his signature had not appeared on the treaty leading many to wonder if he would accept the terms stated or not. He finally did accept them in December 1648 after bowing to pressure from other powers. Regardless of what he managed to regain, regain it he had which was far more of an accomplishment than his father managed during his many attempts to regain control.

Charles Louis remained in England following the signing of the Peace of Westphalia treaty and was there to witness the brutal execution of his uncle, King Charles I. This act left Charles Louis shocked and bereft especially as he had remained unreconciled with his uncle after his refusal to meet with his nephew one last time stating 'my time is short and precious…I hope they will not take it ill, that none have Access unto me but my Children'. At the time of his execution, Charles had with him two of his younger children, Prince Henry, Duke of Gloucester and Princess Elizabeth the other surviving children had made it across to the safety of France and their mother. But it was this lingering in London that led many to believe Charles Louis had designs on the throne, or at least thought he may be offered it, by parliament. Charles Louis left London in March 1649 and returned to the continent but it would take until the September of that year before he finally reached his regained seat at Heidelberg.

Now he was a landed Elector, Charles Louis needed an heir so in February 1650, 33-year-old Charles Louis married the 19-year-old Charlotte Elizabeth of Hesse, a blond beauty considered to be the 'Rose of Hesse'. An heir was born in March 1651 and was quickly followed by a daughter in May 1652. Charles Louis never enjoyed a close relationship with his namesake son; he was a sickly child but he was closer to his precious healthy daughter Elizabeth Charlotte who affectionately became known as 'Liselotte'. A third child was born in May 1653 but he sadly died shortly after birth.

Despite his reinstatement at Heidelberg, Charles Louis refused to allow his mother to join him there but he did invite his siblings to join him. The relationship between mother and son began to deteriorate when he declined her request for financial assistance but he was in no position to offer the help she needed for much of his money was going into repairing Heidelberg castle to bring it back into a habitable residence. Elizabeth demanded access to her dower palaces but again, they needed much repair before they could be made suitable to live in. His mothers letters began to sound desperate and were written with genuine distress and concern:

'I send this by the post to let you know that the States have given me for my kitchen, one thousand guilders a month, till I shall be able to go from hence, which God knows how and when that will be, for my debts. Wherefore I earnestly entreat you to do so much for me to augment that money which you give me, and then I shall make a shift to live a little something reasonable. And you did always promise me that as your country bettered you would increase my means, till you were able to give me my jointure. I do not ask much. If you would add but what you did hint, you would do me a great kindness by it, and make me see you have still an affection for me, and put me in a confidence of it. Since you cannot pay me all that is my due, that will shew you to the world you desire it if you could. I pray you do this for me. You will much comfort me by it, who am in so ill a condition as it takes all my contentment from me. I am making my house as little as I can, that I may subsist by the little I have till I shall be able to come to you.….As you love me, I do conjure you give an answer'

Elizabeth's heartfelt letter is desperately sad to read; here is a lady of such standing who had been brought so low and was having to have to beg her son for help, only for him to refuse her wishes. Unfortunately, these letters were to continue for several years and each time she was rebuffed. Charles Louis's response to his mother's pleading was not the answer she craved. He cruelly told her he would not be paying her creditors and accused her of only writing to him when he had finally returned to Heidelberg.

Charles Louis relationship with his family became strained through the latter 1650s, his mother and siblings felt he should be able to provide financially for them with gifts of money and lands which would then generate revenues for them. What they all failed to realise was that the Thirty Years' War had caused widespread destruction across Heidelberg and if he was to become a respected Elector he needed a seat he could rule from, his funds were depleted but they all still looked to him for financial stability. He was accused by them of being stubborn and set in his ways as well as a miser, unwilling to share the wealth but in reality he did not have enough wealth to share, he must have felt frustrated and angry at their lack of compassion and understanding.

In order to strengthen his ties abroad Charles Louis looked to his children and the dynastic marriages they could make. Firstly, he had to ensure the succession of his line and arranged the marriage of his son Charles to Princess Wilhelmine Ernestine who was daughter of King Frederick III of Denmark. The ceremony took place at Heidelberg on 20 September 1671. The groom was described as being a shy and weak man and his short reign of just five years was as unremarkable as he was. When he died he was debt ridden which would have no doubt angered his father given the hard work he had put in to rebuilding the Lower Palatine. The marriage was unhappy and remained childless meaning when Charles II died on 26 May 1685 at the age of 34 the Electorship of Palatine passed to the House of Palatinate-Neuberg. Given that Charlotte had refused to acknowledge the divorce and therefore block any attempts her husband may have had in siring another male heir meant the only other option available to Charles Louis was to try and persuade Rupert to return to the Lower Palatinate; to marry and have children in the hope one would be a son. Princess Elisabeth tried to help on both counts but sadly failed to persuade either of them to help. What Elisabeth and Charles Louis didn't realise was that Rupert had married in secret in London and was comfortably settled in England and Charles Louis should look elsewhere for his heir because there was no chance of him returning.

Elizabeth Charlotte married just weeks after her elder brother and she made a much grander marriage and one that would be beneficial to her father. Charles Louis had longed been striving for an alliance with the French so he decided to marry his beloved daughter to Philip, Duke of Orléans and the brother of King Louis XIV. This was a marriage which was facilitated by the good connection of his sister-in-law Anna Gonzaga. As part of the marriage negotiations, it was required that Elizabeth Charlotte convert to Catholicism which was an issue neither she nor her father had any qualms with. Once the details had been agreed upon Anna agreed to escort her niece from her home in Heidelberg to Paris. The proxy ceremony took place on 16 November 1671 at the Cathedral of St Stephen in Metz with the Duke of Plessi-Praslin standing in for the groom. Orléans was twelve years older than his bride who was just 19 years old at the time of their marriage. The newly married Elizabeth Charlotte probably had no idea that her husband lived openly as a bisexual and was in a long-term relationship with the Duke of Lorraine as well as having other relationships often with younger men. Despite the circumstances, Orléans knew he had a duty to perform and fathered three children with his wife although after the third was born in 1676 he ended all sexual relations with Elizabeth Charlotte, much to her relief!

Unfortunately, Elizabeth Charlotte had no choice but to accept her husband's way of life but she decided it would not hold her back and she managed to build a close relationship with Louis XIV and throughout the early years of her marriage she fitted into the flamboyant French court with ease. Orléans died of a stroke on 9 June 1701 at the Chateau de Saint-Cloud at the age of 60. Following her husband's death, Elizabeth Charlotte's influence began to dwindle. She had been respected and well-liked but over time she faded away from court. When Louis XIV died on 1 September 1715 it left his 5-year-old great-grandson Louis XV on the throne. Clearly at that age he was too young to rule and so a regent was sought to rule for him until he reached his majority, that man was Phillipe II, Duke of Orléans, Elizabeth Charlotte's eldest surviving son. With her son's new appointment came an elevation in Elizabeth Charlotte's standing and she was elevated back to the heart of court although now she had the freedom to spend her time away from Paris at her own estates in the country.

Through his daughter, Charles Louis created a strong and powerful alliance with France and even though he didn't live to see his grandson rule the country as it's Regent his groundwork placed the Palatine family at the heart of the French royal family, as well as the English.

Charles Louis died on 28 August 1680 aged 60 at Edingen, he may not have gone down in history as being a remarkable man but he had roles to play in the English Civil War and as a grandson of King James VI and I he knew his royal blood meant he had status and he ruled his partially regained lands wisely.

Princess Elisabeth of the Palatine,
Abbess of Herford Abbey

As the eldest daughter of Elizabeth and Frederick, Princess Elisabeth could expect to make a grand marriage. Sadly, and in part thanks to her father's loss of lands and titles, her chances were somewhat diminished when it came to having a choice of groom. Not many powerful men were looking for marriage with a daughter of an exiled king who looked unlikely to regain his lands anytime soon. She did however receive an offer of marriage from Wladyslaw IV Vasa King of Poland in 1633 but the sticking point was that he was a catholic and she was unwilling to convert regardless of how beneficial the marriage might have been to the Palatinate. But Elisabeth was destined for an altogether different life, one that would see her correspond with one of Europe's greatest thinkers and shun marriage in favour of religious orders.

Much of her early life was spent in Brandenberg with her grandmother Louise Juliana of Nassau and aunt Elisabeth Charlotte, Electress of Brandenburg. She stayed there until the time came when all the children of the Palatinate were brought together in The Hague to reside once more with their parents. Along with her siblings, Elisabeth was educated at the Prinsenhof in Leiden where she was taught mathematics, politics, philosophy, science and many various languages. Her intellect and understanding earned her the affectionate nickname of 'La Greque' (The Greek). She was also proficient in painting, dancing and music.

Elisabeth first met French philosopher René Descartes in 1642 when he visited The Hague, and following her return visit to his home near Leiden in 1643, the pair began a correspondence and friendship that would last until his death in 1650. Descartes clearly thought a lot of Elisabeth as he dedicated his *Principles of Philosophy* to her in 1644. He showered her with praise commenting that her intelligence was 'outstanding' with 'incomparable sharpness'. Over a period from 6 May 1643 to 1 July 1643, Elisabeth and Descartes discussed the 'problem of interaction'. She was keen to point out that she did not always agree with the great Frenchman and his way of thinking. This was not because she had anything against him personally but because she felt she learnt nothing new from him. Elisabeth clearly demonstrated a clear Cartesian way of thinking in that one ought to rely on your individual mind in order to speak the truth. Descartes argued that all human beings regardless of intelligence have the capacity for reasoning. He also argued that the body and soul are two separate entities but are joined together none the less. He talked about feeling pain when hurt and hunger when starved such is the connection of the person's soul to the physical body. Despite the distinctions between the two Elisabeth questioned Descartes on his theory in particular if the soul is neither extendable nor can it make physical contact with an object how can it have an impact upon the body and its behaviours? She suggests a more defined explanation on the soul and thought, although distinguishing between the two would be difficult. Naturally, Descartes replied explaining how she had misunderstood his meaning. But it was Elisabeth's belief that if the soul and body are two different entities then they can in no way interact with each other as they have nothing in common.

We have many of Descartes letters that were written to Elisabeth but sadly we do not hold the same number in return for her. She initially refused permission for them to be published in 1657 when French lawyer Claude Clerselier printed Descartes's letters to Elisabeth, she even refused permission for them to be shown to Queen Christina of Sweden. However, her letters were discovered in the nineteenth century hidden away in a library in Arnhem. They were subsequently published in 1879 by French writer Louis-Alexandre Foucher de Careil. Amongst the cache of letters there were 26 written by Elisabeth to Descartes and 33 in reply. Despite the friendship and mutual admiration, Elisabeth was also a critic of Descartes, in particular surrounding his belief that the body and soul are interlinked.

At the time of her mother's death in 1662 Elisabeth had already entered the Lutheran convent in Herford, Germany. Herford was founded in the eighth century and had become the most revered institute for women in Germany. In the twelfth century the Abbey was granted independent status likening it to a small duchy which meant the abbess was responsible for the abbey and the town that surrounded it. Elisabeth was a great correspondent and not only did she nurture a friendship with Descartes but she also had exchanges with prominent Quakers Robert Barclay, William Penn and John Pell who all visited her at Herford. It is said they tried to convert her but she had little interest in talking theology with them, she was steadfast in her religious beliefs and would never countenance conversion. That said, she was always keen to learn of new ideas and theories, hence why she never turned anyone away from the Abbey doors she had always wanted to learn and that desire stayed with her as an adult. In 1659, Elisabeth and her brother, Charles Louis, had a fall-out after she refused to accept Louise von Degenfeld as his wife. When Princess Sophia left Heidelberg to move to Hanover following her marriage, Elisabeth also decided to depart. She initially went to stay with family in Berlin but as she soon realised, she could not stay there forever she needed to decide what the future had in store for her. She was a 40-year-old spinster with little to no financial independence and the only option available to her was the church. Luckily there was a convent just a short distance from Sophia's home and with even better fortune, her cousin, Elizabeth Luise Juliana of the Palatinate- Zweibrücken, was the Abbess.

Thanks to her royal status, Elisabeth would not have been required to enter the order as a nun but she did want a guarantee that the role of Abess would pass to her when her cousin died. In order to help secure her position she put down a payment that she hoped would help persuade other members of the order to vote in favour of her admittance to the Abbey. Unfortunately, they declined Elisabeth's request but she was not to be put off. Instead, she travelled to Herford in October 1660 where she planned to stay for ten days in a bid to win the votes of those who declined her. Whilst she was there, she urged her influential friends to intercede on her behalf. Sadly, all this did was reinforce the order's decision to exclude Elisabeth from the Abbey because to them they felt they were being forced into accepting her based solely on her rank and status rather than her religious convictions. With no one left to turn to she reached out to the overlord of Herford, her kinsman, Frederick William, Elector of Brandenburg, in the hope he would back her cause by threatening to withdraw his financial support of the Abbey until Elisabeth was accepted. It worked as she was finally accepted and joined the order at Herford by the summer of 1661. In 1667, her cousin Elisabeth Luise died and Elisabeth became Abbess, taking the rather impressive title of Princess & Prelatess of the Holy Roman Empire.

Elisabeth's struggles to be accepted into the order were surprising given she was more than qualified for the role. She had been well educated and was clearly an intelligent woman and her upbringing in an exiled court had taught her to be careful with money which gave her the requisite skills to administer the estate. She also had a good knowledge of the outside world; she was well versed in the politics of the day across Europe given her family ties to the court in England and her brother in Heidelberg. Elisabeth's biggest drawback was that she was a Calvinist and Herford Abbey was mostly Lutheran which made the people slightly wary of her, and perhaps they were right to be so. Elisabeth found her subjects less pious than they ought to have been and so set about trying to help them find their way. She was always happy to help those suffering religious persecution but that did not always mean she was popular with the order.

In 1670, the Abbey took in an old acquaintance of Elisabeth, the Dutch painter and author Anna Maria van Schurman along with five male pastors after they had been forced to flee Amsterdam. Schuman had written to Elisabeth requesting sanctuary after suffering religious persecution in Holland. Naturally, Elisabeth willingly opened Herford's gates to them but the townspeople were not as accommodating as their abbess when they learned the new arrivals were not Calvinist or Lutheran in their religious leanings. In fact, they were Labadists, followers of the French pastor Jean de Labadie, a former Jesuit priest turned Protestant leader, Labadie himself was one of the five pastors that accompanied Anna. His followers believed in equality between the sexes, in communal living and who ate and drank freely. It was their belief that the church was not an earthly thing but an entity that was in the fabric of everyday life. Holy Communion was saved for the true believers and members were urged to only pray when they felt the Spirit moved them to do so. The group from Holland had been converted by Labadie himself and Schurman, who was once hailed as the 'Star of Utrecht', had given up everything she owned, and all her material wealth to join the Labadists at the age of 62 years old. Wealth was to be shared amongst the community and no member should have any form of personal riches; everyone was to be equal.

The people of Herford saw the new arrivals as a threat and decided to raise their concerns with the Elector of Brandenburg. They believed Elisabeth had threatened their beliefs and traditions by allowing these foreigners in to their town. For Elisabeth, she felt a huge wave of embarrassment when her guests were verbally attacked in the streets, her argument was that at heart they were true Calvinists, unfortunately that was not what they were preaching. Brandenburg sent his own delegation to meet the Labadists to find out what kind of people they actually were. News of the stand-off between the residents of Herford and the Labadists travelled fast and soon enough Sophia arrived from Hanover to visit her sister as did their nephew Charles, who requested to meet his aunt's guests. The following morning, accompanied by Elisabeth, they were taken to their lodgings where they met Labadie himself, as well as Schurman. They listened patiently to his lengthy sermons, the group argued and debated with each other over various subjects and in a bid to break the cycle Charles requested Labadie speak from a pulpit and to people that were not already indoctrinated into his group so they could assess his finesse for preaching. What they saw and heard did not impress them, they described Labadie as a 'powerless priest' and the 'worst of men'. What shocked them the most however was the number of young, wealthy ladies and children that had shunned their once comfortable lives to follow Labadie. Regardless of what her family thought, and despite a personal visit to speak with Brandenburg, Elisabeth could not win this fight and by the time she had returned from Berlin, Labadie and his followers had decided to leave Herford, much to the joy of the townspeople.

Elisabeth's acceptance and treatment of the Labadists earned her a reputation across Europe of being someone of religious tolerance and before long she was welcoming another persecuted religious group – the Quakers. In the summer of 1677, William Penn visited Elisabeth at Herford. He had previously appealed to her for help when a fellow prominent Quaker had been imprisoned in England for refusing to swear an Oath of Allegiance to the Church of England. Naturally she was more than happy to help where she could. Penn gave up on England and looked towards the continent for new recruits and before long he reached the peaceful town of Herford, and by this time the people had grown to trust and admire Elisabeth. Penn too was impressed with her charitable nature, always making sure there was enough money to ensure the poor were fed and clothed. Despite the issues Elisabeth had faced with the Labadists she still made Herford a religious haven for any pilgrim and was always willing to face the anger of the people. She invited Penn to dine with her so they could discuss the issues he had faced which turned out to be predominantly his parents' displeasure in his choice of religion and the mocking and cruel jibes he had faced at the hands of priests. Elisabeth was never looking to convert and she made this clear to her visitors but she was always ready to listen and learn of other theories and ideas and she listened intently to Penn. She took pity on him, and after listening to him preach the day after she broke down in tears as she had felt so moved by the power of God. Penn would visit Herford again and the friendship that formed between the two would last until Elisabeth's death.

Life continued on peacefully at Herford for the next few years but when in October 1679, Sophia, Electress of Hanover, visited her sister she was shocked to find her emaciated, resembling a skeleton with a distended stomach (Elisabeth was more than likely dying from cancer). As she lay on her death bed, one thing played on Elisabeth's mind and that was her on-going feud with her elder brother Charles Louis. The siblings had remained at odds after Elisabeth supported Charlotte over her brother regarding their divorce and his subsequent marriage to

Louise von Degenfeld. The time had come to face the fact that unless Charles Louis could father another son, the Lower Palatinate was going to leave the family. Elisabeth wrote to Charlotte pleading with her to acknowledge the divorce and let her husband remarry, or, alternatively try and convince Rupert to leave his life in England to return to Germany to marry and have sons. Charlotte declined, and as for Rupert, what Elisabeth and Charles Louis didn't realise was that Rupert had secretly married in London and had children of his own so had no intention of returning to help his brother.

Despite both efforts coming to nothing Charles Louis appreciated the help his sister offered in trying to solve the succession crisis and their relationship thawed to the point that they were once again united before they passed away (Charles Louis would die just six months later). Elisabeth's thoughts then turned to her other sister, Louise Hollandine, a fellow Abbess, albeit a catholic one, and someone she had not seen in nearly thirty years. She wrote to her advising her she was preparing to die and that she hoped to see the face of God for eternity.

Elisabeth, Princess Palatine and Prelatess of the Holy Roman Empire died at the age of 61 on 11/12 February 1680, she was buried in the Abbey Church of Herford.

Prince Rupert of the Rhine,
Duke of Cumberland

Out of all of Elizabeth's children it was Prince Rupert that embraced her homeland more than any other. He was an ardent supporter of his uncle, King Charles I, and when his cousin came to the throne following the restoration of the monarchy in 1660 as Charles II he was by his side to offer a guiding hand. We have already talked about his involvement in the English Civil War and his prowess at leading armies but at the time of his mother's death he was an established member of the English court after having returned in 1660. He was not just a courtier, he was a close family member of the king following the deaths of Princess Mary of Orange and the Duke of Gloucester. So, alongside James, Duke of York he was the king's closet family in England. Charles I had rewarded his nephew for his loyalty by creating him the Duke of Cumberland in 1644 and when he returned to England he took up his place in the House of Lords, Charles II later admitted him to the Privy Council in 1662 (he had been invested as a Knight of the Garter by Charles I in 1645).

Rupert was a natural born soldier and when the second Dutch-Anglo wars (1665–1667) broke out he was appointed a commander of the English fleet. He took HMS *Royal James* as his flagship when he fought alongside the White Squadron in the Battle of Lowestoft in 1665. Unfortunately, his leg was badly injured just as they had managed to breach the enemy lines and so was unable to take any further part. In 1666, Rupert was made joint commander of the fleet alongside General George Monck and in June they engaged the Dutch in the Four Days' Battle, a battle the Dutch claimed victory in the following month. At the St James's Day battle they employed Rupert's new aggressive tactics and managed to destroy the Dutch fleet and claim victory for England. On the 01 September 1666, they engaged in battle again in the North Sea but it did not go as planned. A gale rose up just at the moment the English fleet had manoeuvred into position leading to some of the ships losing their sails, and in some cases even their masts. It also meant they were unable to fire any cannons at the enemy. The king and the Duke of York sat patiently at Whitehall waiting for news on the battle, they would not have been pleased to hear of their failure but by the end of the day they would be brought news that would shatter them. The wind and gales that had risen in the North Sea landed in London that evening and a bakery in Pudding Lane, near London Bridge caught fire. The wind spread the fire across much of the City of London causing utter destruction to the medieval buildings, including St Paul's Cathedral. The Great Fire of London of 1666 brought the King, the Duke of York and no doubt Rupert himself onto the streets where they helped clear away debris, London was to be rebuilt and Rupert was there to see the designs.

In the third Dutch-Angle War (1672–1674) Rupert took command of three ships, the HMS *Royal Charles*, HMS *Royal James* and HMS *Royal Oak*. This war was fought alongside the French which Rupert had openly criticised and that objection cost him the role of Admiral, Charles II appointed his brother James, Duke of York to the role and Rupert returned to the Admiralty. But by 1672 he was back on the water and in command after Charles II realised having his brother and heir in battle was far too risky. The Battle of Schooneveld in the June and the Battle of Texel in August proved disastrous for the Anglo-Franco alliance with bad communication and ill-equipped ships being blamed for the losses. Despite the defeat, Rupert, a dissenting voice from the start, was hailed a hero with the French taking the brunt of the criticism for their lack of engagement during the fighting. Rupert retired from naval duties in late 1673, he was a well-respected military leader and was praised for his energetic approach to battle and the close relationship with his officers which meant his orders were given in a clear and direct manner that successfully filtered down through his men. He became pivotal in the review of tactics and his ideas saw great victories for the fleet. He became closely involved in the fitting out of new ships including the weaponry and personnel needed after Charles II appointed him the leader of the new established Admiralty Commission.

As well as the Admiralty Commission, Rupert also took on roles in the Foreign Affairs Committee and the Tangier Committee, on both he had an active part to play. In 1668, Charles II appointed his cousin as the Constable of Windsor Castle and in true soldiery manner his first job was to strengthen the castles defences and upgrade the garrison living quarters whilst also repairing and maintaining the castles infrastructure. He rebuilt the Real Tennis courts, in fact he was considered in the top five Real Tennis players at court, he also improved the hunting stocks across the estate. Rupert was close with both his royal cousins and this new post meant he spent a lot of time at Windsor with the King and the Duke of York.

In 1664, Rupert became romantically involved with a lady named Frances Bard and together they had a son in 1666 that they named Dudley Bard. There were claims that Frances told people she and Rupert had married in a secret ceremony but this is something he denied and there is no direct evidence to suggest any ceremony took place. Rupert openly acknowledged Dudley as his son and he made sure he was well provided for. He was initially sent to Eton but when he had completed his time there he expressed an interest in following in his father's footsteps and joining the military. To help him achieve this Rupert enlisted Sir Jonas Moore of the Tower of London to instruct him in his military training alongside engineering and mathematics. Dudley's military training was put to use in 1685 when he helped put down Monmouth's rebellion following a skirmish at Norton St Philip. Just a year later on 13 June 1686 he was engaged in battle during the last Christian attack against the Turks at Buda. Sadly, Dudley died not long after aged just 20 years old. Despite his illegitimacy Rupert was fond of his son and when he died, he left him money and his German estates, which were still being held by Charles Louis.

Dudley Bard was not the only child Rupert would have. He embarked on a love affair with the actress Margaret 'Peg' Hughes in 1668. She is often feted as the first ever woman to appear on stage when she performed the role of Desdemona in William Shakespeare's *Othello* on 8 December 1660, prior to this the parts of women were performed by men. It is said that Rupert fell madly in love with her, she was described as being a great beauty and she knew her worth and so fought off his advances long enough for him to offer her all the more luxury. A romance with Prince Rupert brought great advancement for Peg and she was painted by the great court painter, Sir Peter Lely. So great was his love for her many urged him to marry her, even his sister Sophia tried to persuade him to do so, especially following the birth of their daughter Ruperta in 1673. He happily acknowledged her as his child but he declined to marry and remained a bachelor. His generosity grew following Ruperta's birth she and her mother would want for nothing. Peg's love of jewels was more than satisfied and it has been claimed Rupert spent more than £20,000 on her in just over a decade. If he was measuring his love by the amount of money he spent on his lover then Peg was the love of his life. Many cynics saw the relationship as nothing more than an older man falling in lust with a pretty and much younger woman who wanted nothing more than wealth and advancement. When he died, Rupert left most of his possessions to Peg and Ruperta, who was 9 at the time of her father's death. In his will he urged her to obey her mother in all things and when she came to marry she must seek the approval of her mother and the Earl of Craven. Ruperta married Emanuel Scrope Howe in 1695, he was an officer in the army of William III and together they had six children. Ruperta died at Somerset House in 1740 aged 67 years old whilst her mother passed away at the grand age of 89 when she died on 1 October 1719 in Kent.

The military was the most important part of Rupert's life, he was a born soldier and when he retired from active duty in 1674 he was able to dedicate more time to his other passion, science and scientific research. To help perform his experiments he built a custom-made lab at Windsor which he kitted out with all the equipment he needed. Such was his love for science and discovery, Rupert was listed, after his two royal cousins, as a founding member of the Royal Society on 28 November 1660. He has been credited with many inventions including a new device for lifting water at Windsor, but many of his creations were military based including a naval gun he called the Rupertinoe, he also manufactured gun locks and a gun that could fire multiple shots in quick succession. In 1663, he presented a new form of gunpowder to the Royal Society which was said to be at least ten times more powerful than regular gunpowder making it ideal for mining. This list is not exhaustive but it does represent Rupert's technical and enquiring mind.

Prince Rupert of the Rhine, Duke of Cumberland died from pleurisy at his home Spring Gardens off Pall Mall on 29 November 1682, he was 62 years old. His state funeral took place on 6 December and he was laid to rest in Henry VII's Lady Chapel in Westminster Abbey. His tomb inscription reads:

> The remains of the illustrious Prince Rupert, Count Palatine of the Rhine, Duke of Bavaria and Cumberland, Earl of Holderness, Vice-Admiral of all England, Governor of the Constabulary of the Royal Castle of Windsor, Knight of the Most Noble Order of the Garter, Member of the Privy Council of the King's Majesty; third son of the Most Serene Prince Frederick, King of Bohemia etc., by the Most Serene Princess Elizabeth, only daughter of James, sister of Charles I, aunt of Charles the second of that name, both Kings of Great Britain, France and Ireland. Born at Prague, the capital city of Bohemia, on the 17th December 1619, he died in London on the 29th November 1682, in the 63rd year of his age.

Prince Rupert's life has become synonymous with his role in the Civil War during which he showed bravery, courage and unwavering loyalty to stand by his uncle King Charles I. He had energy and flair and was a born fighter always ready to serve his king. Of all of Elizabeth's children he is probably the best known to us.

Princess Louise Hollandine of the Palatine, Abbess of Maubuisson

As mentioned above, Louise Hollandine was omitted from her mother's will due to her unforgivable conversion to Catholicism in December 1657, and Louise's earlier life was never too far from controversy. Described as being pretty with long dark hair, Louise Hollandine had a talent for painting and had received plenty of interest in the marriage market, namely from her cousin Frederick William, Elector of Brandenburg, a match her mother approved of. Feelings at the time were that this was a match made in royal heaven. They were of a similar age, he was a Calvinist and had been the family's most loyal supporter but most of all, Frederick William was in love with Louise Hollandine. Sadly, it was not to be as her family sustained a period of self-destruction. Her uncle Charles I had been deposed and executed in England whilst her brothers fared no better. Philip stood accused of murder whilst Edward had converted to Catholicism in order to marry his French bride and despite having no direct involvement in any of these scandals she was tainted by their association and Frederick William went on to marry Louise Henriette, Princess of Orange.

Louise Hollandine was happy in The Hague as it gave her ample time to sketch and paint whilst providing her with a safe and secure home where she could enjoy intrigue and court gossip. Following her brother's death, Elizabeth's court became a safe haven for displaced royal courtiers and members of the Stuart family and one visitor stood out more than the others. James Graham, Marquis of Montrose was a Scottish nobleman who was loyal to the Stuart cause and was determined to re-establish the monarchy by setting Charles II upon its throne if the young king would only grant him the role of Viceroy of Scotland. Montrose was a brave and courageous soldier and came from one of the highest-ranking noble families in Scotland but he was also a protestant who had managed to withstand pressure from the Presbyterians (Covenanters). This, along with his undying support for Charles I, had made him an enemy of Scotland and in particular Archibald Campbell, 1st Earl of Argyll. Montrose managed to raise a group of soldiers from around his family seat in the Highlands and along with a number of Irish men managed to surprise Argyll and take Perth, unhappy at this, Argyll put a price tag of £20,000 on Montrose's head. When Charles I gave himself up to the Scots, Argyll made the king order Montrose to lay down his weapons and leave Scotland which he did by sailing to France and to the court of Queen Henrietta Maria. When news of Charles's execution filtered across the continent Montrose dedicated his life to avenging the death of his king and the restoration of his son.

In the summer of 1649, he travelled to The Hague where he first met Louise Hollandine and before long he was declaring his love for the beautiful young niece of his former king. He may not have been as high-ranking as Frederick William but before her stood a handsome and courageous man and she fell for him in return. By 22 June, Charles II had ordered Montrose to invade Scotland on his behalf and to hold the country in his name, but before he could leave he returned to Holland to bid Louise Hollandine farewell. He then embarked on a whistlestop tour of Europe gathering allies, supplies and money as he went. Montrose landed on the northern coast of Scotland around 12 April 1650, by which time, everyone in Scotland knew Charles II had ditched him in favour of Argyll and the Covenanters. It turns out the Scots were willing to accept Charles as their king as long as he gave Montrose over to his enemies. The King did not waiver and handed over Montrose's plans to Argyll who now knew when his enemy was coming. Argyll and his men lay in wait for him and finally the attack happened on 27 April at Caithness where many of Montrose's men were taken. By chance he managed to escape with a couple officers but had been badly wounded. After a couple of days of wandering the Scottish countryside, starving and thirsty he came across a farm whose inhabitants fed him bread and milk and gave him a change of clothes which it was hoped would disguise him. Sadly, the disguise didn't work and he was captured just a day later when a labourer spotted him and reported him to the authorities. On 7 May he was captured and paraded down through Scotland dressed in peasant clothes. He was ill from his still bleeding and now infected wounds. He was taken south to Edinburgh where he arrived on 18 May and on the 21st he was taken to the Market Place to face his execution at the Mercat Cross. His hands were tied behind his back and was then hung by the neck until he was dead. He was left swinging for three hours before his corpse was cut down, beheaded and then quartered. His head was placed on a spike at the Tolbooth and his other remains were distributed across Scotland as a warning to others. Given his ranking in Scotland, he ought to have been beheaded as hanging, drawing and quartering was a form of execution usually reserved for thieves and villains of lower ranks of society.

Details of his brutal execution swept across Europe. Louise Hollandine had been at Breda with her mother, sister Sophia and Charles II when the dreadful news reached them. Sophia recorded in her diary that they were 'deeply shocked' at Montrose's 'cruel death'. We have no records of Louise Hollandine's thoughts and feelings over the death of her love or the betrayal of her cousin but I am sure we can try and imagine the hurt and sorrow she must have felt when the news broke that her gallant soldier had been treated in such a way, especially as he was working for the good of the family.

Montrose's death plunged Louise Hollandine into a deep sorrow which was later compounded by the loss of her brother Philip Frederick in battle just six months later which was then quickly followed by the news that Maurice had been lost at sea, presumed dead. The following September she would lose her younger sister Henriette Marie who died just months following her wedding. The hurt caused by the deaths of her loved ones and the political unrest at The Hague following Charles I's execution pushed Louise Hollandine into a decision that she must have been contemplating for some time. She knew she was going to struggle to find a husband and that she would be unable to support herself through painting alone so she had to begin to think of the other options available to her and so she turned to the Church and by the winter of 1657 at the age of 35 she was ready to take the biggest step of her life. With the help of her brother Edward and friend Princess of Hohenzollern she left her rooms in The Hague in the early hours of 19 December and headed to the harbour where a boat was waiting to take her to the princesses home at Bergen op Zoom. From there she would officially convert to Catholicism and retire to a convent in Antwerp. The following morning her mother was handed a letter in which Louise Hollandine declared she was renouncing her Protestant faith to become a Catholic. A further search of her rooms found more letters regarding the escape plans, including the princesses involvement. Angry at her daughter's betrayal, Elizabeth took steps to have her returned to The Hague and to have the Princess brought to account for her role in the plot. It had been insinuated that Louise had to leave as she was pregnant, Elizabeth took this to the Dutch Estates who stripped the princess of some of her privileges, unless she could prove there were no underhand motives involved in Louise Hollandine leaving her home.

Without intentionally doing so, Louise Hollandine now found herself at the centre of a storm of gossip which ran the risk of damaging her reputation beyond repair. Charles II and Princess Mary of Orange visited Louise Hollandine at the convent in Antwerp. Elizabeth then informed Rupert that they had challenged her on her conversion, and she claimed to be satisfied with her choices but regretted the pain she had caused her family. The Bishop of Antwerp confirmed in a letter to Edward that his sister was not and never had been pregnant. From Antwerp, Edward travelled with his sister to Paris, where she was warmly greeted by the 'Sun King' Louis XIV and his queen, Maria Theresa of Spain. On 20 April 1659, Louise Hollandine was officially welcomed into the Catholic Church by the Pope's representative in Paris. The following year she took her vows as a nun at Maubuisson Abbey which sits northwest of the French capital. The Abbey was just as prestigious as Herford, founded in 1241 by Blanche of Castile, queen consort of King Louis VIII and mother of Louis IX. There was a school attached which became a place of education for the children of the highest-ranking members of

French society, including Edward's three daughters. Louise Hollandine's time at the abbey was enriched by her visitors including her aunt, Queen Henrietta Maria, her brother Edward, his wife and daughters, three nieces she had never met before and when the middle daughter Anne married Henri-Julius de Bourbon, Prince de Condé her status at the abbey rose and she became Abbess of Maubuisson just four years after she took her vows. She also met her niece Elizabeth Charlotte, daughter of Charles Louis for the first time after she had married the Duke of Orléans. The two met often and conversed in German sharing stories and discussing painting and the relationship grew into one of mutual respect and love. Elizabeth Charlotte adored her fun-loving aunt and Louise Hollandine declared that she preferred her over her other nieces. Despite her royal connections she lived the true life of a nun including wearing a habit, sleeping on a hard bed and waking in the early hours to pray, although she commented that she didn't mind as the light of the early morning benefitted her as a painter.

In 1679, Sophia visited her sister bringing them together for the first time in thirty years. Sophia commented that her sister was just as happy as ever and describes the convent as being beautiful with large gardens. The sisters got on well and were both upset when they had to part again when the time came for Sophia to return home to Hanover. Louise Hollandine had spent many years trying to convert her sister and painted her a picture from the Old Testament book of Exodus of the Golden Calf.

Louise Hollandine died on 11 February 1709 at the grand age of 86 years old without ever being reconciled with her mother. She never regretted her choice to convert and she led a happy life at Maubuisson Abbey where she was free to paint, see family and friends but at the same time could worship God in the manner she chose.

Prince Edward, Count Palatine of Simmern

Despite his secret marriage, conversion to Catholicism and his help in his sister's conversion Edward managed to gain forgiveness from his mother despite her wishing him dead when she heard the news he had married without her consent. There had been genuine concerns amongst the family that his conversion would pull him away from his Protestant family and the Palatinate cause, but he continued to be a loving son and a loyal brother who supported his family at The Hague, Heidelberg and in England. In fact, he was forced to apologise after publicly insulting Cromwell's agents in the street at The Hague, although in private his mother applauded him for speaking the truth. Sadly, Edward died just a year after his mother aged 37.

Described as being the most handsome of the Palatine princes, Edward had olive skin and dark eyes with thick luscious dark curly hair. His manners were also more refined than his elder brothers which made him a catch for any European princess in the marriage market but it was a lady eight years his senior of Italian and French descent that won his heart.

His marriage to Anne de Gonzaga caused ripples through French society. She had been embroiled in an earlier love affair with Henri de Lorraine (later the Duke of Guise). She claimed the couple had secretly married in 1638 and that Henri had even obtained special dispensation from the Pope given their close familiarity. However, once he became duke he quickly put it about that Anne's claims were false and that the marriage had never taken place at all but Anne continued to call herself the Duchesse de Guise. So adamant that she was in the right, Anne took her case to the Ecclesiastical court in a bid that they would recognise her marriage, unsurprisingly she lost her case and Henri married someone else. Anne did not sit around licking her wounds, instead she went and found herself a handsome young prince to marry. Edward had been studying at the Royal Academy when he first met Anne and no doubt he made a great first impression, they married in secret and then publicly in St Sulpice, Paris.

Anne was a celebrated Parisian beauty who was at the centre of the French social scene. She was well known for holding the finest soirees in the city and if she attended one you had hosted then you really were someone. Despite her marriage she had no intention of giving up this lifestyle, Edward had to fit in with her needs rather than the other way around and that was something he was happy to do. Edward had arrived in Paris penniless, he lived a frugal life but once he had married he suddenly found his circumstances greatly improved. He now found himself travelling in the best coaches and he wore the finest clothes; he never found being a kept men a chore and this was all thanks to his wife's £7,000 (approximately £720,000 in today's money) a year income. Edward and Anne enjoyed a happy marriage with three daughters born to them, all of whom married well and had issue.

Following Charles I's execution, Rupert joined his younger brother in Paris and the two handsome princes enjoyed everything Paris had to offer. The two brothers seemed to enjoy a close relationship no doubt the loss of Maurice hung heavy in the air but that relationship was to turn sour following the death of their mother and it came for her will to be read. Edward made his only visit to England to hear the will be read in person and was left shocked and disappointed at what he found when he got there.

It had been inevitable that Elizabeth would forgive her most handsome son. He never pestered her for money he was polite and courteous and had married well, he even presented his mother with three beautiful granddaughters. She clearly forgave him wholeheartedly as in her will she left him her 'great table diamond'. Edward had requested every letter he had written to his mother, conscious that they contained private family issues that he only ever intended her to read and he did not want them falling into the wrong hands. Rupert, as the executor of the will, couldn't produce them but assured his brother he would have them burned when he did come across them. Edward also declined to accept the diamond his mother had bequeathed him after being sent a receipt to sign to say he had received it, although at this stage Edward had never even seen the diamond, in fact, he wasn't even sure if the diamond existed at all. As his mother's executor, Rupert took control of all her possessions that had not been bequeathed elsewhere. This included her money, plate, jewellery etc. and this angered both Edward and Charles Louis who called into question the validity of the will. This was an inflammatory remark given Rupert had the backing of the king so they were powerless to do anything.

Edward returned to Paris disgruntled at what had transpired but also upset that his brother Rupert could be so callous to his brothers. It was a sad state of affairs that the once happy and loving brotherly relationship had crumbled over money. For Edward it was not even about money, he had never been a money grabber this was about the principle and the slight the Rupert had made against him. We do not know if Edward ever received the 'diamond' or if his relationship with Rupert ever managed to recover before his death on 10 March 1663. Edward died in Paris at the age of 38. Rupert and Charles Louis continued to battle it out for years before finally reaching a settlement in 1667.

It appears that Edward was a very amiable man, he was easy going and seemed a happy, maybe even the happiest of the palatine children. He comes across as a very likeable man but without the pressure of being the heir, like Charles Louis and without the danger of being a soldier like Maurice and Rupert, he managed to strike a good balance and made a successful life for himself which was remarkable given he was a fifth son of an exiled ruler.

Princess Sophia, Electress of Hanover

Out of all of Elizabeth and Frederick's children you could argue that Prince Rupert and his youngest sister Sophia lived the most prominent lives. Rupert was a firm fixture at the courts of Charles I and his son Charles II yet it would be Sophia that provided Great Britain with its new king when the Stuart era ended with the death of Queen Anne in 1714.

Sophia was the youngest of the palatinate princesses and when she was young she enjoyed her fair share of rumour and intrigue. Elizabeth's trusted and loyal advisor William, Earl Craven was at the centre of a plot to marry Sophia to her cousin Charles II because the English wanted a protestant queen and there was no higher protestant princess than Sophia. For her this would have been an amazing match, it would have elevated her to queenship and was far beyond her expectations given she was the fourth surviving daughter of an exiled monarch. The exiled courtiers at The Hague paid particular attention to her when news filtered out that she could be their next queen. The plot quickly unravelled when Charles made attempts to persuade Sophia to get money out of Lord Craven which he could then distribute amongst his friends. Offended at this, Sophia tried to avoid her cousin to save any embarrassment on both parts, much to the frustration of her mother who was in favour of the match.

To put some distance between herself and Charles, Sophia travelled to Heidelberg to visit her brother Charles Louis. The siblings had always enjoyed a close relationship and his recent reinstatement gave her the ideal opportunity to leave the scandal and her mother behind. When she arrived in 1650, Charles Louis had not long married Charlotte, who according to Sophia gave her a frosty welcome leading her to describe her new sister-in-law as being 'very stupid'. It was clear something was wrong between the newlyweds and it did not take long before Sophia became the shoulders on to which they both unburdened themselves. Charlotte told her she had married Charles Louis against her will and that he was nothing but a jealous old man. As with many young women of the time she had turned down other princes and dukes to please her family and now she was trapped in a loveless marriage. Charles Louis claimed that whilst his wife was young and beautiful and very wealthy she had been raised poorly and it had been left to him to direct her on what was appropriate and what was not. It was no wonder that this marriage would eventually fail and given she did not want to marry him in the first place it is perhaps also understandable why Charlotte refused him his divorce, she must have felt like nothing but a pawn to be moved around at the will of the men in her life. The marital strife caused upset for Sophia and she quickly wanted leave and return home to The Hague but she knew that was not an option so she did the next best thing she could and invited her sister Elisabeth to Heidelberg to share the burden of their brother and his unhappy wife.

Given that her two elder sisters took holy orders attention soon switched to Sophia and her future. Duke Ernst Augustus of Hanover had been suggested by his own brother George William; it was he that Sophia had been betrothed to but she released him from his obligation when he declared he wished to remain a bachelor. So, Ernst Augustus took his brother's place as Sophia's bridegroom as well as the town of Lüneburg which George William ceded to his younger brother. The wedding took place on 17 October 1658 in Heidelberg and they seemed a perfect match; he was just a month shy of his twenty-ninth birthday whilst she had just celebrated her twenty-eighth. The bride wore a gown of silver brocade and a diamond encrusted crown which sat majestically on her head as her long hair fell loosely down her back. She was escorted down the aisle by her brothers Charles Louis and Edward and as the happy couple said 'I do' the cannons from the castle fired across the city in celebration. Following the ceremony the guests were treated to a lavish supper followed by a ball with dancing and music. Several days later

Ernst Augustus left Heidelberg and travelled home to Hanover in order to oversee preparations for his brides arrival.

Sophia arrived at the Hanoverian court a few days after her husband, here she met the finest of society and in order to please them a second marriage ceremony took place. The early days of their marriage in Hanover were blissful, they enjoyed each other's company and quickly became devoted to each other. Unfortunately, things quickly became difficult as George William was also staying at court and he took more than a passing interest in his new sister-in-law. He would follow her and position himself next to her at every opportunity, was he ruing his mistake in passing Sophia over to his brother? Ernst Augustus certainly thought so and a row erupted between the newlyweds with Ernst Augustus accusing Sophia of preferring his brother over him, an accusation she flatly denied. She managed to convince her husband that it was he she loved and there was never any suggestion she had behaved improper with George William. Before long Ernst Augustus forgave the pair but he remained suspicious.

Tradition was that Ernst Augustus and George William would visit Italy every winter and by the winter of 1659, Sophia was pregnant with her first child. Ernst decided his wife ought to not undertake such a journey given her condition so Sophia, and her niece Elizabeth Charlotte, went to The Hague to stay with Elizabeth. On 28 May 1660, Sophia gave birth to her first child, a son named George. The delivery was difficult but thankfully mother and baby thrived.

Heavily pregnant with her second child, Sophia travelled to Rotterdam to say goodbye to her mother who was finally returning home to England. On the 2 October 1661, a second son was born to Sophia and Ernst Augustus and shortly after that Ernst Augustus was appointed the Prince-Bishop of Osnabrück which greatly improved the family's finances and status. Ernst Augustus was a committed Lutheran but it had been agreed as part of the Peace of Westphalia the position would alternate between Catholic and Protestant, the district fell under George William's jurisdiction but he chose to appoint his younger brother to the illustrious role. The family relocated to Iburg Castle but it was simply not big enough so work began on a much grander residence, Osnabrück Palace. Ernst

Augustus's new position also bought a new title for Sophia; she became known as the Bishopess and in her role she would have been expected to attend church regularly and tend to charitable causes for the poor and sick.

In April 1664, Sophia joined her husband and brother-in-law on their annual trip to Italy, the children were left at Heidelberg in the care of Charles Louis. She was not keen on the trip, unlike her husband who was eager to make the journey south, but just what exactly was he so keen on? Like most aristocratic men of the seventeenth century, he had taken a mistress and spent most of his evenings in Italy entertaining her whilst Sophia was left alone. Whilst she was in Rome, Sophia had a private audience with Pope Alexander VII but it was not long before she was leaving the Italian capital and returning home. In the spring of 1665, Ernst Augustus escorted his wife to the gates of Rome in his carriage, once he had seen out her out of the city and on her way home, he returned to the carriage and to his mistress. His delay in returning home meant he was out of the country when his eldest brother Christian Louis, Duke of Brunswick-Lüneburg died at Celle on 15 March 1665. Duke John Frederick, the third brother seized his elder brother, George William's, property and titles much to the anger of Ernst Augustus who rushed home when he heard the news of his brother's passing. When he arrived in Hanover he immediately offered his support to George William, who as the eldest surviving brother, ought to have inherited the dukedom. Ernst Augustus threated military action against his brother in support of another, unsurprisingly, John Frederick backed down and the duchy of Celle passed to George William whilst the duchy of Hanover was transferred to John Frederick and as a reward for his loyalty, George William handed his younger brother the county of Diepholz.

On 13 December 1666, Sophia gave birth to a third son, Maximillian William at Iburg. Just two years later she gave birth to her only daughter Sophia Charlotte and she was quickly followed by the birth of another son, Charles Philip who arrived on 13 October 1669. On 29 September 1671, another son was born who was named Christian Henry, she had her final child another son at Iburg Castle on 7 September 1674 who was named for his father, Ernest Augustus. Children at this time often perished in infancy and this did not discriminate as Sophia had to endure the trauma of giving birth to still born twins in February 1664 and again in 1666 the twin of Maximillian was also stillborn. Sophia and Ernst Augustus quite rightly wanted their eldest son George to inherit the Hanoverian lands and title but when John Fredrick married Sophia's niece Benedicta Henrietta in November 1667 it became worryingly apparent that if she gave birth to a son it would potentially disinherit George and his siblings. The baby race was on and Sophia performed her duty exceptionally well by providing Ernst Augustus with six healthy sons, all they had to do was hope Benedicta Henrietta did not conceive a son. John Frederick was 27 years older than his wife and had lived a lavish lifestyle and as a result he died at the age of 54 on 18 December 1679 He and his wife had four daughters, with three surviving to adulthood. John Frederick's property and titles passed to Ernst Augustus, making Sophia the Duchess of Hanover.

The family relocated to Hanover and the court grew in size as it took on the former members of John Frederick's court and government who wished to retain their places. One of the men who had been in charge of the library and correspondence was Gottfried Wilhelm Leibniz, a giant in the field of mathematics and philosophy. Sophia made a good impression on him calling her 'a great genius' and the pair soon struck up a close friendship enjoying many philosophical debates together. One of the most ambitious projects they worked together on was the unification of Catholics and Protestants given the fundamental Christian beliefs they both shared and agreed on. Sophia encouraged Leibniz on many of his ideas including the mapping out of Ernst Augustus's ancestry, something he took a great interest in. There was however one idea she did not agree with and that was the plan to consolidate the families lands into one entity and thereby creating a ninth electorship – Hanover. In doing this Ernst Augustus would be disinheriting his younger sons as everything would pass down to George as the eldest son. Unsurprisingly, the five youngest sons were loud in their opposition and refused to sign the documentation that would disinherit them. In retaliation, their father withdrew all financial support and threw them out of the family home.

It was all in vain because in 1692 Leopold I, Holy Roman Emperor appointed Ernst Augustus as the Elector of Hanover and Sophia the Electress. She loved all her children equally and shed tears for her sons and the very fact that five of them were in direct conflict with their father must have been very difficult for her to accept. Sadly, Sophia no longer held any influence over her husband as she once had and that waned even further when he installed his mistress, Clara Elisabeth, Countess von Platen-Hallermund, in a grand house and decked her out in fine clothes and even finer jewellery.

In December 1680, the 20-year-old George travelled to England with a view of marrying Princess Anne, daughter to the James, Duke of York (later King James II). Rupert was living in London and took his nephew on board and made the necessary introductions at court, this was also a match Rupert openly supported. Things were going well, George and Anne seemed to get on, he even kissed her on the lips, with the permission of Charles II, but his visit coincided with a Catholic uprising and he witnessed the beheading of Lord Stafford and that put an end to any further negotiations, he packed his bags and returned home immediately. The marriage of George was of importance and soon he was being matched to his cousin Sophia Dorothea daughter of George William and his morganatic wife and long-term mistress Eleonore d'Esmier d'Olbreuse. It was clear that all the family's estates would eventually be inherited by George given none of the other brothers had sired a son, so George William was keen for this match. The match did not sit well with Sophia given the young lady's lineage, she saw her as illegitimate and therefore not an eligible match for her son. There was also the issue that Sophia did not like her sister-in-law Eleonore, she found her sly and devious and as it turned out she had been working undercover to arrange a marriage with son of the Duke of Wolfenbüttel without the knowledge of the wider family. Sophia was asked by Ernst Augustus to visit Celle to arrange the marriage between the cousins, it didn't take much to persuade George William but Eleonore was furious that her plan had been usurped and she had no power to change it. She had been expecting to announce the engagement that morning at Sophia

Dorothea's sixteenth birthday breakfast which the Wolfenbüttel's were attending. When the news broke that Sophia Dorothea was in fact engaged elsewhere they turned around and left, without eating a morsel of the lavish breakfast. Sophia Dorothea had been brought up by her mother to resent her cousin George, she had been spoilt by her parents as they doted on their only precious child, George William always ceded to his daughters pleas, but not this time, regardless of how much she protested against the match, she was to marry George.

The wedding took place on 21 November 1682, neither was thrilled at the match but George understood the need to marry where his parents thought best. Their first child, a son called George, was born 30 October 1683, a daughter followed on 26 March 1687 and she was named Sophia Dorothea. The marrying of aristocratic children was a political minefield and next up on the marriage carousel was the much-loved daughter Sophia Charlotte, as the only daughter with six brothers she was close to her mother and Sophia had big ambitions for her. The chosen man was the eldest son of the Elector of Brandenberg, Frederick. The pair were married in a spectacular ceremony at Herrenhausen, Sophia's private residence outside the city walls of Hanover.

Across Europe power was shifting, in April 1688, the Elector of Brandenberg died making Frederick and Sophia Charlotte the new Elector and Electress. The next shocking news came from England and the overthrowing of King James II in favour of his daughter and son-in-law who took the throne as Queen Mary II and King William III.

The marriage between George and Sophia Dorothea had begun to deteriorate quickly and when he confronted her about alleged rumours that she was having an affair she demanded a divorce and fled home to her parents in Celle but they quickly returned her to George. The rumours were not unfounded as Sophia Dorothea had been conducting an affair with Philip Christoph von Königsmarck, a Swedish count, and the two had been plotting their escape. Sadly, their plans were foiled and Ernst Augustus gave the order that he ought to be arrested and so sent guards to his rooms, but something went wrong and it is assumed that he was murdered. Whatever happened that evening no one saw or heard from

Königsmarck again although during routine renovations at Leineschloss in 2016, bones were found under the floorboards, tests reveal that there were several people buried there, perhaps one of them was Königsmarck. Sophia Dorothea was distraught and panic stricken over what may have befallen her lover, after a thorough search of his rooms many love letters were discovered between the two and distributed to Ernst Augustus, Sophia, George and her parents. Sophia Dorothea was charged with desertion on 28 December 1694 and confined to house arrest at a castle in the remote village of Ahlden, north of Hanover. Legend has it that her young son George managed to escape from Hanover and ran to Ahlden and swam across the castle's moat in a bid to reach his mother. The young George hated his father for what he had done and in return the father began to despise the son and there started a long line of Hanoverian British kings hating one another. Sophia Dorothea stayed there for her remaining thirty-two years in total isolation; she was permitted to see her mother on occasions but she never saw her children again.

Sophia's world changed forever on 23 January 1698 when her husband of forty years, Ernst Augustus died at Herrenhausen. Better news came in January 1701 when Sophia Charlotte's husband, Frederick, was crowned King Frederick I of Prussia, finally Sophia saw her daughter take a crown and become a queen.

On 22 June 1701, a law was passed in England called the Act of Settlement and contained within the act was the law that the crown could only be passed to a Protestant, the next Protestant in line after Princess Anne was Sophia, Electress of Hanover, it read:

be enacted and declared and be it enacted and declared by the Kings most Excellent Majesty by and with the Advice and Consent of the Lords Spirituall and Temporall and Commons in this present Parliament assembled and by the Authority of the same That the most Excellent Princess Sophia Electress and Dutchess Dowager of Hannover Daughter of the most Excellent Princess Elizabeth late Queen of Bohemia Daughter of our late Sovereign Lord King James the First of happy Memory be and is hereby declared to be the next in Succession in the Protestant Line to the Imperiall Crown and Dignity of the forsaid Realms of England France and Ireland with the Dominions and Territories

A copy of this was presented to Sophia by an English Delegation in Hanover. Following her husband's death, Sophia, now aged 73, lived a quiet life at Herrenhausen. She had lost her sons Frederick Augustus and Charles Philip to war and in 1703 she lost Christian who was shot whilst fighting against the French in Bavaria but in 1705 she would endure the agony of losing her beloved daughter Sophia Charlotte. The Prussian queen had been in Hanover but died unexpectedly on 2 February when she caught pneumonia, Sophia had not been able to visit her daughter as she herself was ill in bed with a heavy cold which prevented her from seeing her daughter one last time.

By the summer of 1714, Sophia had fallen ill and during a leisurely walk she felt faint from pains in her stomach, her ladies tried to get her back to the main house but they were caught in a heavy downpour and were only able to get her to a small covered seating area. Sophia collapsed in her ladies arms claiming 'I am very ill: give me your hand' those would be the last words she ever spoke as she fell unconscious dying a short while later. Sophia, Electress of Hanover and heir to the British throne was 83 years old when she died in her beloved gardens at Herrenhausen, she was originally buried in the chapel at the Elector's Palace, Hanover however, following the destruction of the palace in World War Two, Sophia, Ernst Augustus and their eldest son George were relocated to a mausoleum in the gardens at Herrenhausen.

Two months later on 1 August 1714, Queen Anne of Great Britain and Ireland died at Kensington Palace meaning Sophia's eldest son George ascended the throne as King George I and at that point the Hanoverian, or Georgian as it is otherwise known, period began. King George I was crowned at Westminster Abbey on 18 October 1714 and that marked the start of a royal dynasty that still sits on the throne today.

At this stage we should also remind ourselves that Elizabeth had lost six of her children prior to her own death. Prince Frederick Henry, Prince Maurice, Prince Louis, Princess Henriette Marie, Prince Philip Frederick,

Princess Charlotte and Prince Gustavus Adolphus. They were all taken too young and we can only imagine the great things they could have achieved had they lived to adulthood. There is often a misconception that women of Elizabeth's rank, and of the time, had little interest in their children, that they were a necessary burden they had to go through in order to prolong their dynastic lines. And whilst Elizabeth is often described as being cool and somewhat stand-offish in her parenting style she would have mourned deeply for each one of her lost children.

Elizabeth Stuart's Descendants

We know that Sophia's eldest son became King George I of Great Britain but what of Elizabeth Stuart's other grandchildren? Did they marry well? Just how far across Europe did Elizabeth's legacy reach? Below is a brief outline, not all the grandchildren are named for some had many children but I have picked out the highlights that show us how influential the Palatine princes and princesses were in the marriage market.

Charles Louis's son Charles II died without issue but his daughter Elizabeth Charlotte, who I have already briefly mentioned, married Philippe I, Duke of Orléans and together they had three children, two of which survived to adulthood. The son, Philippe d'Orléans married his cousin Francoise Marie de Bourbon and together they had eight children and seven of them reached adulthood. Six of them married, Louise Adelaide became the Abbess of Chelles. Another daughter Louise Elizabeth married Louis I, King of Spain although she only reigned alongside him for seven months following his death at 17 from smallpox. The marriage was later annulled by Louis's father following strange and abnormal behaviour on Elizabeth's part. Elizabeth Charlotte and Philippe's youngest child was a daughter name Elizabeth Charlotte and she made a marriage to Leopold, Duke of Lorraine and together they had fourteen children although sadly many died in infancy. Their eldest surviving son was Francis and made a grand marriage to Archduchess Maria Theresa of Austria, daughter of the Holy Roman Emperor. Their marriage was hugely successful and together they had sixteen children and one of those was a daughter named Archduchess Maria Antonia, when she married she became known as Marie Antoinette, the last Queen of France. So not only does Elizabeth's blood run through the British royal family, it also ran down to one of history's most famous queens.

Edward and Anne had three daughters who all married and had issue. Louise Marie married Charles Theodore, Prince of Salm and together they had one son, Louis Otto and three daughters. The youngest surviving daughter was Eléonore Christine and she married Conrad Albert, Duke of Ursel and had issue. Edward's second daughter, Anne Henriette, married Henri-Julius, Prince of Condé on 11 December 1663 at the Palais de Louvre, Paris with the royal family in attendance. Sadly, this was not a happy marriage, he was mentally unstable and often beat his quiet and submissive wife but she supported him, realising he was ill and his violent rages were not necessarily under his control. Despite the nature of their marriage, they had ten children together, with five surviving to adulthood, out of those five, four married into the French aristocracy with the eldest son Louis de Bourbon marrying Louise, the daughter of the king. The youngest daughter was Benedicta Henrietta and she married John Frederic, Duke of Brunswick-Lüneburg and together they had four children, two of which married. Their eldest daughter Charlotte Felicitas married Rinaldo d'Este, Duke of Modena and had six children, the youngest being Wilhemina Amalia and she married Joseph I, Holy Roman Emperor and their daughter Maria Amalia married Charles II, Holy Roman Emperor.

By the time Sophia died in 1714 she had only two of her sons still living, George came to England and his youngest brother Ernest Augustus took on the role of head of the family back home in Hanover. He took on the role of Prince-Bishop of Osnabrück just as Ernst Augustus had and so split his time between that role and his commitments in Herrenhausen. In the summer of 1716, Ernest Augustus decided to visit his brother in England and to reward him for his loyalty the king created him Duke of York and Albany and Earl of Ulster and just two years later, alongside his grand-nephew and future Prince of Wales, Frederick, was created a Knight of the Garter.

It is clear from the above that the grandchildren of Elizabeth and Frederick married well. Each of them strengthened what had come before and it was only the First World War that saw the face of Europe change forever that many of the monarchies they had married into ended.

The French monarchy suffered a spectacular fall from grace in January 1793 with the execution of King Louis XVI. Great Britain and King George III looked on in terror lest the revolutionary thoughts travel across the channel. Thankfully they didn't but George III would have troubles of his own.

After The Stuarts

King George I was crowned at Westminster Abbey on 18 October 1714 and that marked the start of a royal dynasty that still sits on the throne today.

At the centre of the royal circle sat Elizabeth Stuart a link from the old world of Tudor England to the glamorous world of the Hanoverian court. The granddaughter of Mary, Queen of Scots in turn became the grandmother of the first Georgian king of Great Britain and Ireland over 127 years later. Her children and grandchildren married well stretching her bloodline throughout Europe to the royal houses of Prussia, Great Britain and France.

On 16 October 1793, Marie Antoinette climbed the scaffold at the Place de la Concorde in the centre of Paris to face her execution by the guillotine. She was following in the footsteps of her 6x great-grandmother Mary, Queen of Scots who faced her executioner at Fotheringhay Castle just over 200 years earlier. Two queens who struggled to gain the love of their people, two women who were misunderstood and two mothers who left kings behind to rule in their wake, although tragically 10-year-old Louis XVII was a king in name only and died following his imprisonment and neglect at the hands of his jailors. They were two women who are held together by blood ties all linked through Elizabeth Stuart, the Winter Queen.

In England, the Hanoverian dynasty saw the beginnings of a constitutional monarchy as power shifted away from the crown and to Parliament and the country's first Prime Minister Sir Robert Walpole. A move that brought political stability to the country. It was also a time that saw the British Empire begin to grow and the Industrial Revolution sweep across the nation both of which would reach their peak during the reign of George I's great-great-granddaughter, Queen Victoria.

The era, otherwise known as the Georgian period, saw the face of the nation change. The rise of the middle-class and the growth of towns and cities saw building expand and the architecture known for its symmetrical line and sash windows brought the emergence of the elegant town houses set around squares such as Bloomsbury and Mayfair in London and the grand crescent in Bath. People began to read novels with the emergence of Jane Austen and Jonathan Swift; poets such as Lord Byron and William Wordsworth wrote romantic poems that made them the rockstars of the age. Gone were the stiff clothes of the Tudor and Stuart age and in their place came grand elaborate gowns and high unnatural hairstyles for women whilst the men donned powdered wigs and breeches. By the reign of the unpopular and vain George IV, clothes had become more relaxed and comfortable.

All these changes, and those since, can all be traced back to Elizabeth, her descendants have changed the face and fabric of this nation and despite her having lived much of her life on the Continent her impact should not be under estimated or over looked.

The Solemn League and Covenant

For reformation and defence of religion, the honour and happiness of the King, and the peace and safety of the three kingdoms of Scotland, England, and Ireland; agreed upon by Commissioners from the Parliament and Assembly of Divines in England, with Commissioners of the Convention of Estates and General Assembly of the Church of Scotland; approved by the General Assembly of the Church of Scotland, and by both Houses of Parliament, and the Assembly of Divines in England, and taken and subscribed by them Anno 1643; and thereafter, by the said authority, taken and subscribed by all ranks in Scotland and England the same year; and ratified by act of the Parliament of Scotland Anno 1644. (And again renewed in Scotland, with an acknowledgement of sins and engagements to duties, by all ranks, Anno 1648, and by Parliament, 1649; and taken and subscribed by King Charles II., at Spey, June 23, 1650; and at Scoon, January 1, 1651.)

WE noblemen, barons, knights, gentlemen, citizens, burgesses, ministers of the Gospel, and commons of all sorts, in the kingdoms of Scotland, England, and Ireland, by the providence of GOD living under one king, and being of one reformed religion, having before our eyes the glory of God, and the advancement of the kingdom of our Lord and Saviour JESUS CHRIST, the honour and happiness of the king's majesty and his posterity, and the true public liberty, safety, and peace of the kingdom, wherein every one's private condition is included: and calling to mind the treacherous and bloody plots, conspiracies, attempts, and practices of the enemies of GOD, against the true religion and professors thereof in all places, especially in these three kingdoms, ever since the reformation of religion; and how much their rage, power, and presumption, are of late, and at this time, increased and exercised, whereof the deplorable state of the Church and kingdom of Ireland, the distressed state of the Church and kingdom of England, and the dangerous state of the Church and kingdom of Scotland, are present and public testimonies: we have now at last (after other means of supplication, remonstrance, protestation, and sufferings), for the preservation of ourselves and our religion from utter ruin and destruction, according to the commendable practice of these kingdoms in former times, and the example of GOD'S people in other nations, after mature deliberation, resolved and determined to enter into a Mutual and Solemn League and Covenant, wherein we all subscribe, and each one of us for himself, with our hands lifted up to the Most High GOD, do swear,

I.   THAT we shall sincerely, really, and constantly, through the grace of GOD, endeavor, in our several places and callings, the preservation of the reformed religion in the Church of Scotland, in doctrine, worship, discipline, and government, against our common enemies; the reformation of religion in the kingdoms of England and Ireland, in doctrine, worship, discipline, and government, according to the Word of GOD, and the example of the best reformed Churches; and shall endeavour to bring the Churches of GOD in the three kingdoms to the nearest conjunction and uniformity in religion, Confession of Faith, Form of Church Government, Directory for Worship and Catechising; that we, and our posterity after us, may, as brethren, live in faith and love, and the Lord may delight to dwell in the midst of us.

II.   That we shall, in like manner, without respect of persons, endeavour the extirpation of Popery, Prelacy (that is, Church government by archbishops, bishops, their chancellors and commissioners, deans, deans and chapters, archdeacons, and all other ecclesiastical officers depending on that hierarchy), superstition, heresy, schism, profaneness, and whatsoever shall be found contrary to sound doctrine and the power of Godliness; lest we partake in other men's sins, and thereby be in danger to receive of their plagues; and that the Lord may be one, and his name one, in the three kingdoms.

III.   We shall, with the same sincerity, reality, and constancy, in our several vocations, endeavour, with our estates and lives, mutually to preserve the rights and privileges of the Parliaments, and the liberties of the kingdoms; and to preserve and defend the king's majesty's person and authority, in the preservation and defence of the true religion and liberties of the kingdoms; that the world may bear witness with our consciences of our loyalty, and that we have no thoughts or intentions to diminish his majesty's just power and greatness.

IV. We shall also, with all faithfulness, endeavour the discovery of all such as have been or shall be incendiaries, malignants, or evil instruments, be hindering the reformation of religion, dividing the king from his people, or one of the kingdoms from another, or making any faction or parties among the people, contrary to this League and Covenant; that they may be brought to public trial, and receive condign punishment, as the degree of their offences shall require or deserve, or the supreme judicatories of both kingdoms respectively, or others having power from them for that effect, shall judge convenient.

V. And whereas the happiness of a blessed peace between these kingdoms, denied in former times to our progenitors, is, by the good providence of GOD, granted unto us, and hath been lately concluded and settled by both Parliaments; we shall, each one of us, according to our place and interest, endeavour that they may remain conjoined in a firm peace and union to all posterity; and that justice may be done upon the willful opposers thereof, in manner expressed in the precedent article.

VI. We shall also, according to our places and callings, in this common cause of religion, liberty, and peace of the kingdoms, assist and defend all those that enter into this League and Covenant, in the maintaining and pursuing thereof; and shall not suffer ourselves, directly or indirectly, by whatsoever combination, persuasion, or terror, to be divided or withdrawn from this blessed union and conjunction, whether to make defection to the contrary part, or to give ourselves to a detestable indifferency or neutrality in this cause, which so much concerneth the glory of God, the good of the kingdom, and honour of the king; but shall, all the days of our lives, zealously and constantly continue therein against all opposition, and promote the same, according to our power, against all lets and impediments whatsoever; and what we are not able ourselves to suppress or overcome, we shall reveal and make known, that it may be timely prevented or removed: All which we shall do as in the sight of God.

And, because these kingdoms are guilty of many sins and provocations against GOD, and his Son JESUS CHRIST, as is too manifest by our present distresses and dangers, the fruits thereof; we profess and declare, before GOD and the world, our unfeigned desire to be humbled for our own sins, and for the sins of these kingdoms; especially that we have not, as we ought, valued the inestimable benefit of the Gospel; that we have not laboured for the purity and power thereof; and the we have not endeavoured to receive Christ in our hearts, not to walk worthy of him in our lives; which are the causes of other sins and transgression so much abounding amongst us: and our true and unfeigned purpose, desire, and endeavour, for ourselves, and all others under our power and charge, both in public and in private, in all duties we owe to GOD and man, to amend our lives, and each one to go before another in the example of a real reformation; that the Lord may turn away his wrath and heavy indignation, and establish these Churches and kingdoms in truth and peace. And this Covenant we make in the presence of ALMIGHTY GOD, the Searcher of all hearts, with a true intention to perform the same, as we shall answer at that great day, when the secrets of all hearts shall be disclosed; most humbly beseeching the LORD to strengthen us by his HOLY SPIRIT for this end, and to bless our desires and proceedings with such success, as may be deliverance and safety to his people, and encouragement to other Christian Churches, groaning under, or in danger of the yoke of antichristian tyranny, to join in the same or like association and covenant, to the glory of GOD, the enlargement of the kingdom of JESUS CHRIST, and the peace and tranquillity of Christian kingdoms and commonwealths.

Appendix Two

The Act of Settlement 1700 (Passed in 1701)

The below document sets out the order of succession following the death of Queen Anne of Great Britan.

<u>The Act of Settlement 1700 (passed in 1701)</u>
Recital of Stat. 1 W. & M. Sess. 2. c. 2. §2. and that the late Queen and Duke of Gloucester are dead; and that His Majesty had recommended from the Throne a further Provision for the Succession of the Crown in the Protestant Line. The Princess Sophia, Electress and Duchess Dowager of Hanover, Daughter of the late Queen of Bohemia, Daughter of King James the First, to inherit after the King and the Princess Anne, in Default of Issue of the said Princess and His Majesty, respectively and the Heirs of her Body, being Protestants.

Whereasin the First Year of the Reign of Your Majesty and of our late most gracious Sovereign Lady Queen Mary (of blessed Memory) An Act of Parliament was made intituled [An Act for declaring the Rights and Liberties of the Subject and for setling the Succession of the Crown] wherein it was (amongst other things) enacted established and declared That the Crown and Regall Government of the Kingdoms of England France and Ireland and the Dominions thereunto belonging should be and continue to Your Majestie and the said late Queen during the joynt Lives of Your Majesty and the said Queen and to the Survivor And that after the Decease of Your Majesty and of the said Queen the said Crown and Regall Government should be and remain to the Heirs of the Body of the said late Queen And for Default of such Issue to Her Royall Highness the Princess Ann of Denmark and the Heirs of Her Body And for Default of such Issue to the Heirs of the Body of Your

Majesty And it was thereby further enacted That all and every Person and Persons that then were or afterwards should be reconciled to or shall hold Communion with the See or Church of Rome or should professe the Popish Religion…should be excluded and are by that Act made for ever to inherit possess or enjoy the Crown and Government of this Realm and Ireland and the Dominions thereunto belonging or any part of the same or to have use or exercise any regall Power Authority or Jurisdiction within the same And in all and every such Case and Cases the People of these Realms shall be and are thereby absolved of their Allegiance And that the said Crown and Government shall from time to time descend to and be enjoyed by such Person or Persons being Protestants as should have inherited and enjoyed the same in case the said Person or Persons so reconciled holding Communion professing…as aforesaid were naturally dead After the making of which Statute and the Settlement therein contained Your Majesties good Subjects who were restored to the full and free Possession and Enjoyment of their [Religion] Rights and Liberties by the Providence of God giving Success to Your Majesties just Undertakings and unwearied Endeavours for that Purpose had no greater temporall Felicity to hope or wish for then to see a Royall Progeny descending from Your Majesty to whom (under God) they owe their Tranquility and whose Ancestors have for many Years been principall Assertors of the reformed Religion and the Liberties of [Europe] and from our said most gracious Sovereign Lady whose Memory will always be precious to the Subjects of these Realms And it having since pleased Almighty God to take away our said Sovereign Lady and also the most hopefull Prince William Duke of Gloucester (the only surviving Issue of Her Royall Highness the Princess Ann of Denmark) to the unspeakable Grief and Sorrow of Your Majesty and Your said good Subjects who under such Losses being sensibly put in mind that it standeth wholly in the Pleasure of Almighty God to prolong the Lives of Your Majesty and of Her Royall Highness and to grant to Your Majesty or to Her Royall Highness such Issue as may be inheritable to the Crown and Regall Government aforesaid by the respective Limitations in the said recited Act contained doe constantly implore the Divine Mercy for those Blessings And Your Majesties said

Subjects having Daily Experience of Your Royall Care and Concern for the present and future Wellfare of these Kingdoms and particularly recommending from Your Throne a further Provision to be made for the Succession of the Crown in the Protestant Line for the Happiness of the Nation and the Security of our Religion And it being absolutely necessary for the Safety Peace and Quiet of this [Realm] to obviate all Doubts and Contentions in the same by reason of any pretended Titles to the [Crown] and to maintain a Certainty in the Succession thereof to which Your Subjects may safely have Recourse for their Protection in case the Limitations in the said recited [Act] should determine Therefore for a further Provision of the Succession of the Crown in the Protestant Line We Your Majesties most dutifull and Loyall Subjects the Lords Spirituall and Temporall and Commons in this present Parliament assembled do beseech Your Majesty that it may be enacted and declared and be it enacted and declared by the Kings most Excellent Majesty by and with the Advice and Consent of the Lords Spirituall and Temporall and Comons in this present Parliament assembled and by the Authority of the same That the most Excellent Princess Sophia Electress and Dutchess Dowager of Hannover Daughter of the most Excellent Princess Elizabeth late Queen of Bohemia Daughter of our late Sovereign Lord King James the First of happy Memory be and is hereby declared to be the next in Succession in the Protestant Line to the Imperiall Crown and Dignity of the [said] Realms of England France and Ireland with the Dominions and Territories thereunto belonging after His Majesty and the Princess Ann of Denmark and in Default of Issue of the said Princess Ann and of His Majesty respectively and that from and after the Deceases of His said Majesty our now Sovereign Lord and of Her Royall Highness the Princess Ann of Denmark and for Default of Issue of the said Princess Ann and of His Majesty respectively the Crown and Regall Government of the said Kingdoms of England France and Ireland and of the Dominions thereunto belonging with the Royall State and Dignity of the said Realms and all Honours Stiles Titles Regalities Prerogatives Powers Jurisdictions and Authorities to the same belonging and appertaining shall be remain and continue to the said most

Excellent Princess Sophia and the Heirs of Her Body being Protestants And thereunto the said Lords Spirituall and Temporall and Commons shall and will in the Name of all the People of this Realm most humbly and faithfully submitt themselves their Heirs and Posterities and do faithfully promise That after the Deceases of His Majesty and Her Royall Highness and the failure of the Heirs of their respective Bodies to stand to maintain and defend the said Princess Sophia and the Heirs of Her Body being [Protestants] according to the Limitation and Succession of the Crown in this Act specified and contained to the utmost of their Powers with their Lives and Estates against all Persons whatsoever that shall attempt any thing to the contrary.

Appendix Three

Key Battles of the Thirty Years' War

The Thirty Years' War spanned the majority of Europe and many battles were fought and lives lost. The Spanish forces were led by Don Ambrosio Spinola and Johan Tzerclaes, Count of Tilly and Don Gonzalo Fenandez de Cordoba. They were able to take advantage of Frederick's precarious situation by invading the Protestant German Palatinate in 1620. By 1622 the Palatinate had been lost to Spain.

Listed below are the battles that primarily affected the Palatinate cause. The Bohemian phase of the war took place between 1618–1625.

The Battle of Pilsen, 24 May 1618, Pilsen, Czech Republic (a later siege lasted from 18 September – 21 November 1618)

The Battle of White Mountain, 8 November 1620, Prague, Czech Republic

The Capture of Oppenheim, 14 September 1620, Germany

The Siege of Jülich, 05 September 1621 – 03 February 1622, Germany

The Battle of Mingolsheim, 27 April 1622, South of Heidelberg

The Battle of Wimpfen, 06 May 1622, Germany

The Battle of Höchst, 20 June 1622, Frankfurt, Germany

The Siege of Heidelburg, 23 July – 19 September 1622, Heidelburg

The Siege of Mannheim, 02 November 1622, Germany

The Battle of Stadtlohn, 06 August 1623, North Rhine-Westphalia

The Siege of Frankenthal, 1621 – 20 March 1624, Germany

The Siege of Breda, 1624–1625, Germany

The below battles were fought with involvement from Frederick V, Elector Palatine.

The Battle of Breitenfeld, 17 September 1631, Leipzig

The Battle of Rain, 15 April 1632, Bavaria

Bibliography

Ackroyd, P. *Civil War: The History of England Volume III*, (Pan, London, 2015)

Akkerman, N. *Elizabeth Stuart: Queen of Hearts*, (Oxford University Press, Oxford, 2021)

Ashley, M. *A Brief History of British Kings and Queens: British Royal History from Alfred the Great to the Present*, (Robinson, London, 2016)

Borman, T. *Crown & Sceptre: A New History of the British Monarchy from William the Conqueror to Elizabeth II*, (Hodder & Stoughton, London, 2021)

Cogswell, T. *James I, Penguin Monarch Series*, (Penguin Books, London, 2019)

Curzon, C. *Sophia: Mother of Kings: The Finest Queen Britain Never Had*, (Pen & Sword History, Barnsley, Yorkshire, 2019)

Ericson Wolke, L. *Gustavus Adolphus, Sweden and the Thirty Years War, 1630 1632*, (Pen & Sword Military, Barnsley, Yorkshire, 2002)

Dale, I. *Kings & Queens: 1200 Years of English & British Monarchs*, (Hodder & Stoughton, London, 2023)

Doran, S. *From Tudor to Stuart: The Regime Change from Elizabeth I to James I*, (Oxford University Press, Oxford, 2024)

Fraser, A. *The Gunpowder Plot: Terror & Faith in 1602*, (Phoenix, London, 2002)

Fraser, A, *Mary Queen of Scots*, (Phoenix, London, 2002)

Fraser, S. *The Prince Who Would Be King: The Life and Death of Henry Stuart*, (William Collins, London, 2018)

Goldstone, N. *Daughters of the Winter Queen: Four Remarkable Sisters and the Enduring Legacy of Mary, Queen of Scots*, (Weidenfeld & Nicolson, London, 2018)

Hadlow, J. *The Strangest Family: The Private Lives of George III, Queen Charlotte & the Hanoverians*, (William Collins, London, 2015)

Kishlansky, M. *Charles I Penguin Monarch Series*, (Penguin, London, 2018)

Kitson, F. *Prince Rupert: Portrait of a Soldier*, (Constable, London, 1994)

Jackson, C. *Devil-Land: England Under Siege 1588–1688*, (Penguin Books, London, 2022)

Lincoln, M. *London & the 17th Century: The Making of the World's Greatest City*, (Yale University Press, USA, 2021)

Massie, A. *The Royal Stuarts: A History of the Family that Shaped Britain*, (Jonathan Cape, London, 2010)

Morrah, P. *Prince Rupert of the Rhine*, (Constable, London, 1976)

Oman, C. *Elizabeth of Bohemia*, (Hodder & Stoughton, London, October 1938)

Pike, J. *The Thirty Years War, 1618 – 1648: The First Global War and the end of Habsburg Supremacy*, (Pen & Sword Military, Barnsley, Yorkshire, 2025)

Purkiss, D. *The English Civil War: a People's History*, (Harper Perennial, London, 2007)

Ross, D, Scotland: *History of a Nation*, (Lomond Books, Edinburgh, 2013)

Russell, G. *Queen James: The Life and Loves of Britain's First King,* (William Collins, London, 2025)

Spencer, C. *Killers of the King: The Men Who Dared to Execute Charles I,* (Bloomsbury, London, 2015)

Spencer, C. *Prince Rupert: The Last Cavalier,* (Phoenix, London, 2007)

Spencer, C. *To Catch a King: Charles II's Great Escape,* (William Collins, London, 2018)

Thomson, G M. *Warrior Prince: The Life of Prince Rupert of the Rhine,* (Secker & Warburg, London, 1976)

Tillyard, S. A *Royal Affair: George III and his Troublesome Siblings,* (Vintage, London, 2007)

Turnbull, M, *Charles I Private Life,* (Pen & Sword History, Barnsley, Yorkshire, 2023)

Turnbull, M. *Prince Rupert of the Rhine: King Charles I's Cavalier Commander,* (Pen & Sword Books LTD, Barnsley, Yorkshire, 2025)

Uglow, J. *A Gambling Man: Charles II & the Restoration,* (Faber & Faber, London, 2009)

Veerapen, S. *The Wisest Fool: The Lavish Life of James VI & I,* (Birlinn, Edinburgh, 2023)

Weir, A. *Mary Queen of Scots: And the Murder of Lord Darnley,* (Vintage, London, 2008)

Wilson, P H. *Europe's Tragedy: A New History of the Thirty Years War,* (Penguin, London, 2010)

Winn, J A. *Queen Anne: Patroness of the Arts,* (Oxford University Press, Oxford, 2014)

Online Resources
https://www.schloss-heidelberg.de/en
https://www.english-heritage.org.uk/learn/histories/the-english-civil-wars-history-and-stories
https://www.legislation.gov.uk/aep/Will3/12-13/2
https://www.rmg.co.uk
https://www.archives.parliament.uk/online-resources/proceedings-and-journals/
https://www.heraldica.org/topics/orders/garterlist.htm

Index